YOU ARE
A
THEOLOGIAN

JEN WILKIN
& J. T. ENGLISH

YOU ARE
— A —
THEOLOGIAN

AN INVITATION TO KNOW
AND LOVE GOD WELL

B&H
PUBLISHING
BRENTWOOD, TENNESSEE

Contents

INTRODUCTION   What a Generation Forgot   1

CHAPTER 1   Why Does Theology Matter?   15

CHAPTER 2   Who Is God?
               The Doctrine of the Trinity   29

CHAPTER 3   What Is God Like?
               The Attributes of God   51

CHAPTER 4   What Is the Bible?
               Revelation: The Doctrine of Scripture   63

CHAPTER 5   Who Are We?
               Anthropology: The Doctrine of Humanity   83

CHAPTER 6   What Went Wrong?
               Hamartiology: The Doctrine of Sin   103

CHAPTER 7   What Has God Done? (Part 1)
               The Doctrines of Christology, Atonement,
               and Justification   119

CHAPTER 8   What Has God Done? (Part 2)
              *Pneumatology: The Doctrine of the
              Holy Spirit*   139

CHAPTER 9   To Whom Do We Belong?
              Ecclesiology: The Doctrine of the Church   159

CHAPTER 10   How Does the Story End?
              Eschatology: The Doctrine of Last Things   181

Conclusion: Made You Look   201
About the Authors   205
Acknowledgments   207
Notes   209

What a Generation Forgot

This book exists to serve the part of the Great Commission a generation of church leaders forgot. When we think of Jesus's command in Matthew 28 to go and make disciples, we tend to assign it to the category of evangelism. We picture Jesus's disciples fanning out across the known world armed with gospel tracts or a hand-sketched diagram showing the sin gap that separates us from God, and a cross to span that gap. We picture joyful conversions followed by joyful baptisms. And then we picture those evangelists moving on to the next town, carrying the gospel from Jerusalem to Judea to the ends of the earth.

But if our understanding of the Great Commission is primarily a call to evangelism, we have forgotten a key piece of what it requires:

"Go, therefore, and make disciples of all nations, baptizing them in the name of the Father and of the Son and of the Holy Spirit, *teaching them to observe everything I have commanded you.*" (Matt. 28:19–20, emphasis added)

Jesus's final command is not a call to make converts, but a call to make disciples. And as the Great Commission states, that call will require us to teach converts to *observe all that has been commanded.* Arguably, we have no power to make converts. But making disciples? According to Jesus, we are to replicate ourselves by passing along the good deposit that was passed along to us.

In one sense, the Great Commission is not new when we hear it uttered by Jesus. It sounds a great deal like David's claim that "one generation will declare your works to the next and will proclaim your mighty acts" (Ps. 145:4). It sounds a lot like Moses's exhortation to Israel:

These are the commands, decrees and laws the LORD your God directed me to *teach you to observe* in the land that you are crossing the Jordan to possess, so that you, your children and their children after them may fear the LORD your God as long as you live by keeping all his decrees and commands that I give

2

you, and so that you may enjoy long life. . . .
These commandments that I give you today
are to be on your hearts. Impress them on
your children. Talk about them when you sit
at home and when you walk along the road,
when you lie down and when you get up.
Tie them as symbols on your hands and bind
them on your foreheads. Write them on the
doorframes of your houses and on your gates.
(Deut. 6:1–2, 6–9 NIV, emphasis added)

A disciple is a learner. In the Great Commission, as in
Deuteronomy 6, those who are more mature in the faith are
called to teach those who are less mature, training them into
the core beliefs of the faith. Discipleship is both a skill and a
discipline (as the term *disciple* indicates), requiring effort and
commitment, as all worthwhile skills do.

Conversion happens in an instant. Discipleship, on the
other hand, is the work of a lifetime. It involves the transmission of an ancient faith from one generation to the next.

So, how are we doing with that?

According to most indicators, not great. In 2022, Lifeway
Research and Ligonier Ministries partnered to release a report
on the state of theology in the church. They surveyed both
Christians and non-Christians on their understanding of
basic Christian theology, the essential beliefs that define who

is a Christian and who is not. The results among non-Christians were predictably dismal, but it's the results among professing Christians that are particularly alarming. Consider just a few of the findings:

- God learns and adapts to different circumstances: **48%** of evangelicals agree
- Everyone is born innocent in the eyes of God: **65%** of evangelicals agree
- God accepts the worship of all religions, including Christianity, Judaism, and Islam: **56%** of evangelicals agree
- Jesus was a great teacher, but he was not God: **43%** of evangelicals agree (up from **30%** in 2020)[1]

Let that sink in. Professing Christians in staggering numbers don't understand or ascribe to the most basic beliefs of the faith they claim to stake their lives on. They lack basic theological understanding. And the trends show that the knowledge gap is not getting better, but worse. It would appear that one generation has failed to tell the next. It would appear that we have made converts, but not disciples.

How did we get here? If a disciple is a learner, a discipler is a teacher. But we cannot teach what we ourselves have never been taught. We cannot transmit to another generation what has not been transmitted to us. And we will not aspire to teach anyone else the basic beliefs of our faith if we do not consider ourselves primarily as disciplers. We must learn to think of ourselves from a different angle. We must see ourselves not merely as evangelists or as mentors or as casual participants in a system of belief. We must see ourselves as theologians.

J. T.'s Story

I will never forget my first theology class in seminary. It would be hard for me to overstate how intimidated I was. Not only am I not a great student (I was accepted into college under academic probation), but now I was entering into a field of study I knew nothing about. I didn't grow up in the church, so things like the Bible, theology, and church history seemed like they were for superspiritual Christians. Don't get me wrong; I certainly wanted to grow—that's why I was there—but I still didn't know if I belonged. To me, theology just seemed like old books, lots of footnotes, and words I had to look up.

As I sat down in that first class, all kinds of questions were racing through my head: *Am I smart enough to do this? Is the material going to be way over my head? Will I walk out of these doors embarrassed? Should I be making this kind of investment of time and resources into something I know nothing about?* Every question centered around this idea: *Do I even belong here?*

I felt so out of place. In the classroom, there were about a hundred students buzzing around with excitement. From my perspective, they all appeared to be so confident, so eager, so prepared and excited to be there. As I sat toward the back of the class, thoughts of inadequacy were piling on. *Is it possible that God just wants me to have a simple faith and leave the theology to the experts? After all, Peter and John were uneducated and common disciples, but people knew they were followers of Jesus (Acts 4:13). I would settle for that description of me: uneducated, common, but with Jesus.*

Right then, the professor walked into the classroom.

The buzz that once filled the room quickly went silent. He carried himself with a sense of gravity that matched his extremely credentialed academic background. He introduced himself by showing us pictures of his family and talking about his interests and hobbies. We quickly began to read through the syllabus as he discussed our various writing assignments, books that we would read, a group project, and expectations that he was going to hold us to.

To put it bluntly, I was ready to walk out. *I cannot do this*, I thought. It is one thing to have syllabus shock, but it is another thing to have syllabus shock when the topic is God Himself. Instead of walking out, I decided to simply let the class finish so I would not call attention to myself.

After we finished going through the syllabus, the professor took a blue dry-erase marker and walked over to the whiteboard. He slowly wrote one word on the whiteboard: *theology*. He turned around and asked the classroom to define the term. A few brave students began to answer. One student said, "The study of the Bible." Another student said, "History of Christianity." One more student proposed, "A study of truth."

After several more attempts, the professor drew a horizontal line through the word *theology*, kind of like this: theo | logy. He then said, "Theology is simply words about God."

That seemed like too simple of a definition. Theology is just words about God? It has to be more than that, right? He began to teach us that the Greek term for God is *theos* and the Greek term for word is *logos*. Therefore, *theos* + *logos* = theology, or words about God.

Then he asked us the question, "Who has words about God?" Just like before, some brave students began to answer. One student said, "Pastors and ministry leaders." Another student said, "Professors and academics." The professor seemed to nod in agreement, but then he said, "Who else?"

The room was silent again. Who else does theology other than pastors, ministry leaders, professors, and professional academics? I'll never forget what the professor said next. Very quietly, he said, "Everybody."

Everybody? How can everybody be a theologian?

I know I'm not a theologian. I know my wife is not a theologian. I know my parents are not theologians. How can everyone be a theologian? If I am already a theologian, then why do I need to go to seminary. I came to seminary so that I could become a theologian, not because I already am a theologian.

He continued to explain that everybody has words about God. Certainly pastors, ministry leaders, and professors have words about God, but so do moms, dads, lawyers, health-care professionals, Hindus, Buddhists, even agnostics and atheists. Everyone has words about God; therefore, everyone is a theologian. The question is not whether we are theologians but whether we are good ones or bad ones.

He then asked every single student to stand up and repeat after him: "My name is _____ and I am a theologian."

The first time we tried it, there were a few giggles, and certainly a lack of confidence for most of us.

He then said, "Let's try that again with a little more confidence. Repeat after me: 'My name is _____ and I am a theologian.'"

The second time through it felt a bit more natural to all of us. I said with confidence, "My name is J. T. English, and I am a theologian."

Ever since that day, I have thought about myself a little bit differently. No matter what my vocation is, no matter how young I am or how old I am, no matter my family situation, my income level, or my geographical location, I will always be a theologian.

Jen's Story

I have an English degree. That's it. I didn't attend Bible college. I didn't attend seminary. I got an English degree because I loved language. I won spelling bees and essay contests my whole academic life, and I can diagram sentences as a professional sport. Unfortunately, no one wants to watch that on ESPN. I am a grammarian, complete with hot takes about the Oxford comma and the proper use of *lay* and *lie*. And I can attest to the fact that everyone is a grammarian, but not necessarily a good one. Everyone is obeying rules of grammar, but some of us are using the wrong rules. If you don't know the proper usage of the verbs *lay* and *lie*, you're one of those people. And I'm judging you so hard.

But even in my grammatical dogmatism, I can concede that not much is at risk when those rules are not observed. The same cannot be said of theology. Everyone is a theologian, and the better we are at it, the more this world functions as it was designed to.

While J. T. was discovering he was a theologian and growing in his ability to operate as such, I was floundering around in my local church trying not to teach error, unsure of where I should turn for help.

First, I taught seventh-grade Sunday school. I had grown up in the church, so I tried to replicate what had been done for me when I was in seventh grade. We used a workbook to

9

go through the Gospel of John. Was it a good workbook? I had no idea. Based on the (flawed) premise that all contact with the Bible was good contact, I forged ahead.

Next, I was unexpectedly asked to teach a women's Sunday school class. That's when the panic set in.

I was twenty-nine, younger than everyone else in the class, and I had no blueprint. I also had no training and way less life experience than my students. They were divorced, widowed, married to unbelievers. They had suffered infertility, the loss of children and spouses, physical and emotional suffering. They were battling fears and sins I couldn't relate to, and my life looked dramatically uncomplicated by comparison to theirs. With no training and no battle scars to speak of, what on earth could I possibly teach them that wouldn't seem flippant or fraudulent?

We started slogging our way through the One-Year Bible, but each week's reading posed more questions than it answered. My husband, Jeff, had begun listening to a radio show during his commute called *Renewing Your Mind* by R. C. Sproul. Dr. Sproul referenced Louis Berkhof's *Systematic Theology*, and Jeff gifted it to me for my thirtieth birthday.

Everything changed. Pregnant with my fourth child and with three others under the age of four, I devoured doctrines during naptime and evenings. If the kids were asleep and I was awake, I was probably reading. All of a sudden, I discovered categories I had never known for the ideas I could see in Scripture. And apparently, these categories were not new—they were just new to me. I read Berkhof, and I started reading R. C. Sproul. I mined his footnotes for other authors, and a world opened up to me that I had not known existed.

My Sunday school class became a place I could connect different doctrines to the passages of Scripture we were reading that week. I began to feel more competent, and my confidence as a teacher grew. Whereas I had previously thought the role of a Bible teacher was to build a new teaching out of thin air, now I realized it was to transmit old and time-tested teachings to new ears. Through the centuries, others had built a reliable framework for how to think about God, and that framework was available to me. I could make it available to those I taught.

In all of this, not once did I think of myself as a theologian. Berkhof? Yes. Sproul? Obviously. All those voices I found in the footnotes? Theology giants. I, on the other hand, was a lay leader in a corner of the local church no one paid attention to, teaching a demographic no one expected much from, with no formal training and none on the horizon.

Two decades later, I still don't have formal training. But I know this with certainty: *I am a theologian.*

And I want *you* to know it too. All of us have words about God. We can grow in our ability to make those words accurate and good, edifying for others, glorifying to the One they describe. Not only are we all theologians, but we are so by design. We were created to think and speak words about God that represent Him rightly. We are built for theological thought and discourse—every last one of us. I'm still not the theologian I should be, but I'm working on it.

And I'm inviting you to do the same. Whether you share words about God around a dinner table, in a Sunday school classroom, at a coffee shop, in a workplace, or on a social media platform, you can grow in your fluency. And God will yield a harvest from your efforts.

Your Story

The Great Commission calls disciples to make disciples. What is a disciple? A theologian learning to be a Christian theologian. A person with words about God learning to have true words about God and to live in light of them.

Maybe you picked up this book with a major sense of impostor syndrome. Maybe you picked it up out of sheer curiosity. Or maybe out of desperation because you feel ill-equipped to do the work the Lord has given you to do. We want to help.

This book has two primary goals. The first is for you to see yourself, and everyone else, as a theologian. We want you to perceive your role in worshipping and proclaiming the one true God. We want you to understand yourself as someone who has been invited into the Christian task of thinking and living in accordance with who God is. Because if you can understand that, you will be ready to take your place in the Great Commission call to make disciples.

Our second goal is for you to grow in your knowledge and love of God through theology. God is an inexhaustible well of beauty, riches, and glory. Theology invites us into beholding and enjoying Him as such. We want to convince you that all of life is ultimately about theology because all of life is lived in reference to who God is, who we are, what He has done, and what He is doing. It is our love for God that fuels our desire and our efforts to tell the next generation. We teach others because to remain silent is unimaginable, so marvelous is this God we know.

As you can tell by now, this book is coauthored. It's coauthored by two friends—two friends who've learned how to do theology together. We have learned separately, learned from each other, and have agreed or disagreed with each other depending on the day and the topic. That's how theology is supposed to work. Both of us will share stories in our own voices, and when we do that, we will make it clear. Otherwise, we have written this book together with one voice. That's because we share a mission to catalyze Christians in all contexts and all around the world to awaken to their identity as theologians—as faithful disciples of Jesus Christ. We have worked shoulder to shoulder in both local and parachurch spaces to build and replicate equipping ministries so that this generation of believers would not be panicked but prepared to pass along the good deposit to the next.[2]

This book is, in large part, the result of that work. It will teach you basic theology, but more than that, it is an invitation into lifelong contemplation, celebration, worship of, and service to the one true God. Because even after you read the last page, the joyful task of theology will have just begun. Theology is meant to be the work of your lifetime, one in which you are not merely a consumer of but a contributor to the conversation about God.

Since that's the case, take your pen and fill in the blank:

"My name is _____ and I am a theologian."

Now, read that sentence out loud. How does it feel? It's a statement that has always been true of you in one way or another. Let's ensure it is true of you in a way that marks you as a disciple of Christ, a theologian who patterns their heart, soul, mind, and strength after Jesus of Nazareth.

A book cannot make you a theologian because *you already are a theologian*. Be the best one you can.

The next generation of disciples is waiting to be formed. The church of tomorrow needs good, faithful, humble theologians today. They are waiting for you.

Welcome to the conversation. Welcome to the mission.

CHAPTER 1

Why Does Theology Matter?

Theology is words about God. You are a theologian. Be a good one.

We have posed some basic definitions and challenges, but perhaps you're not yet convinced theology really matters. Why not just stick to the Bible? What, exactly, is the relationship between the Bible and theology? When we set out to study theology, are we adding to God's Word and complicating what is straightforward?

If you're not asking these questions, you should be.

To help answer them, we can look to the Bible for help. In particular, we can look to the examples of two key figures: Adam and Jesus. In the creation account of Genesis 1, we see God bring order to the world, populating the sea, skies, and land. We know His creation is one way that God reveals Himself to us. We can look at what is made—mountains, sunsets, hummingbirds—and know something of His unseen attributes (Rom. 1). But God does something worth noting in Genesis 1:28: He charges the man and woman to take up and continue the work of bringing order to the world.

> God blessed them, and God said to them, "Be fruitful, multiply, fill the earth, and subdue it. Rule the fish of the sea, the birds of the sky, and every creature that crawls on the earth."

And immediately in chapter 2 we see Adam do exactly that. God brings all of the animals to Adam to be named, to be taxonomized, as it were.

He does not say, "Let there be a new species of hippopotamus." No, the work of creation is finished. Rather, he says, "Here is a hippopotamus, and here is a water buffalo." He does not add to God's creation; Adam simply brings organizing language to what already exists. In doing so, he is bearing the image of an orderly God. And he is fulfilling the command God has given him to take dominion.

You do similar things, as well. You probably use a calendar to keep your meetings and other commitments in view. Maybe you have bought organizer bins to arrange your socks and T-shirts in your closet or the items in your pantry. Maybe you own a labeler that makes you very happy. Maybe you've developed a filing system to keep your files in order. All of these organizational efforts do not add to what is being organized; they simply make those items accessible and useful. In a small way, you are bringing about order as you were created to do.

Like taxonomies, organizer bins, filing systems, and calendars, theology is a means of organizing the ideas given to us in God's Word. Theology does not add to those ideas; it simply gives us a way to understand them comprehensively from Genesis to Revelation. Theology sorts ideas into categories, it provides helpful labels, it orders relationships and events from a high-level view.

We see Jesus do the ordering work of theology in a famous scene that occurs after His resurrection. In Luke 24, we find two disciples walking on the road to Emmaus trying to make sense of all that has just occurred in Jerusalem. Jesus greets them, though they do not recognize Him, and He asks them what they are talking about. They recount the confusing events that have occurred since His crucifixion. Luke notes that Jesus responds in this way:

> He said to them, "How foolish you are, and
> how slow to believe all that the prophets have
> spoken! Wasn't it necessary for the Messiah to
> suffer these things and enter into his glory?"

> Then beginning with Moses and all the
> Prophets, he interpreted for them the things
> concerning himself in all the Scriptures.
> (Luke 24:25–27)

In response to their confusion, Jesus gives these two disciples a theology lesson. On a seven-mile walk that would have taken a little over two hours, He teaches them the doctrine of Christ. They knew the Old Testament prophecies. What they needed was a high-level view. He gives them an organizational lens on revelation they already had. Just as Adam brought order to natural revelation, Jesus brings order to the special revelation of the Old Testament writers.

When we do theology, our task is not to add to what God has revealed in the Scriptures, but to order it. Theology is a way to organize and better know and understand what God has gifted us in special revelation.

Why Does Theology Matter?

Theology matters because it shapes us not merely at the intellectual level, but at the emotional and the practical level. One of the greatest misconceptions about theology is that it is something learned in a classroom or through reading a book. Christians do not merely learn theology; they "do theology." The grammarian in Jen does not love this phrase, but it is commonly used for a reason. It communicates the holistic impact of theology on our lives: we think differently, feel differently, and act differently as a result of developing better categories for understanding God.

Theology is not done exclusively or even primarily in the classroom. It is done in everyday life, every minute of every day. We are doing theology when we preach, pray, and sing, but we are also doing theology when we go to work, when we take a vacation, as we care for an aging parent, as we fight sin, as we raise kids, as we mourn the loss of a loved one, as we spend our money, and as we grow old. You are a theologian, and you are always doing theology.

"Theology for Academics"

If this is true, then doing theology is a consequential endeavor. Why, then, do many avoid taking up the task of getting better at it? One common hurdle is the perception that theology is overly academic. To be honest, sometimes it can be, but that doesn't mean it can't also be accessible. Because academics do theology at a level some of us never will doesn't mean all of us should avoid doing theology altogether. Most of us will never get a PhD in applied mathematics, but we still benefit from learning math beyond a rudimentary understanding for the purpose of conducting our everyday lives well. Theological concepts can and should be accessible to everyone: kids, parents, young professionals, people with PhDs or GEDs.

"Theology Is Impractical"

A second obstacle is the perception that doing theology is impractical. Everyone wants to live a life that makes sense. We want to give our lives to what matters most. This isn't true for Christians only; it's true for all people—just look at how impassioned people are about the causes they support, their political convictions, and even their favorite sports teams. Put simply, we all want to be a part of something bigger than ourselves, and we want our lives to matter. If theology is simply words about God, and God is the most important being—the ultimate Reality—is there anything that matters more? And, for that matter, is there anything more practical? If theology is understanding who God is and orienting our lives to that, is there anything more important for us? There is nothing more practical than a life well lived, and theology is a means to that end.

"Theology Is Heartless"

A third obstacle is the perception that theology emphasizes thinking, not feeling. This is true in part. It is more accurate to say that theology begins with the mind and moves to the heart. Doing theology is the work of mind renewal for the purpose of heart transformation (Rom. 12:2). Christianity is not a religion of the mind only—some cold, dead, and dusty intellectual exercise. But neither is it a religion of the heart only—all emotion and fervor, and no reasoned belief.

Theology does not worship the life of the mind, but rather acknowledges that "the heart cannot love what the mind does not know."[3] Theology fails if it is an intellectual exercise only. Theology functions properly if an enlivened intellect fuels an enlivened heart. It recognizes the beauty of reason in the life of faith, and it gives to reason a vocabulary and a vision. Thinking deeply about God should always result in feeling deeply about God. Theology that does not lead to doxology (worship) is not theology at all, but a vain pursuit of knowledge. What's the difference? The motive of the learner and the work of the Holy Spirit in applying what is learned.

So, is theology academic? It can be. But it is meant to be accessible to all disciples. Is theology impractical? Far from it. In fact, knowing and loving God well is the most practical thing in the world. Does theology lack feeling? Not at all. True theology always leads to loving and worshipping God.

> What is theology? *Words about God.*
> Who does theology? *Everybody.*
> What does theology do? *It organizes biblical truths.*

Why does theology matter? *Because living
well matters.*

Simply put, theology is part of a life well
lived. *Theology helps us live all of life well.*

How Do We Do Theology?

Where do we start? Theology is done *biblically, prayer-
fully, worshipfully, humbly, and together in community.*

First, theology must be *biblical.* The aim of Christian theology is to reflect on God's revelation of Himself in Scripture.
Theology that is not a reflection of Scripture ceases to be
Christian theology. Christian theologians pattern their words,
thoughts, and worship around who God says He is and what
He has done as revealed in Scripture. Disciples of Jesus never
graduate from Scripture. We never move past it. We never get
bored with it. Scripture is the lifeblood of theology. We return
to Scripture over and over again, so that we may know and
commune with God. He meets us there. He reveals Himself
there. He speaks to us there. The Bible is our primary authority because in Scripture God makes Himself known to us.

Not only must theology be biblical, but it also must be
prayerful. Theology begins and ends with prayer. The task of
theology is best done on our knees, asking God, by the power
of the Spirit, to awaken our hearts and minds to the person
and work of Christ in the Scriptures. In prayer, we begin to

see God and ourselves rightly. We have the opportunity to attend to God as our Creator and Redeemer, and we ask Him to help us, His creatures, with the task of theology. We ask the Holy Spirit to illuminate our darkened hearts and minds so we can know God truly. Prayerless theology is likely prideful intellectualism. We can't know God unless He makes Himself known to us, which is why we pray. In the matter of theological growth, let it never be said of us that we did not have because we did not ask.

Theology is also meant to be *worshipful*. It is not meant to make us love theology more, but to love God more. Theology is distinctly relational, not drearily informational. In current Christian subculture, it is sometimes reflected that knowledge just puffs up. Any intellectual expression of faith veers dangerously toward the example of the Pharisees. In short, too much thinking will kill worship. But theology and worship are not adversarial. They are two sides of the same coin. Theology is loving God with our minds. Theology is meant to lead us into greater worship of God, and worship of God is meant to lead us into greater knowledge of God. Doctrine and doxology fuel each other. Everything we learn about God should yield worship of God.

Theology is also meant to be a work of *humility*. Theologians never strut. Fundamentally, a disciple is a learner. Everything you have ever learned required humility in the process because anything worth learning requires practice to become proficient. With theology, we are doing more than simply learning a skill. We are humble theologians because we cannot know God unless He makes Himself known to us. All knowledge of God is given by God. It is an act of grace for God to make Himself known to us. To know God is to know grace. Therefore to know God is to grow in humility. There is no room for pride in theology. A prideful theologian is a contradiction of terms. All theology is meant to be marked by Spirit-driven humility. If your theology is leading you into pride, throw it away and get a better theology. If your theology is leading you to deeper humility, then keep pressing forward because you are being transformed into the image of Christ, which is the goal of all theology.

Last, but certainly not least, theology is not meant to be done alone but together, in *community*. And by community, we mean both our contemporary communities and the historic church. God has given you a context, a community, and relationships for a reason. God is calling you to engage theologically in your relationships. Spouses, brothers and sisters, parents and children, neighbors, and friends are called into the task of theology together.

In the context of the local church, we are able to learn about God from other people in our immediate setting, and they from us. There is no such thing as a lone-ranger theologian. When we do theology together, we are testifying to the God-ordained truth that we need one another. None of us is sufficient for the theological task as an individual, but when we come together to do theology, we learn from one another. Men, women, young, old, various socioeconomic backgrounds, and diverse ethnicities—we help one another by learning from one another.

In the context of the global church, we are able to learn about God from our contemporaries in widely different cultural settings than ours. Different life experiences contribute to different vantage points and lenses through which we see the Scriptures. We're all looking at the same beautiful gospel diamond, but brothers and sisters from different parts of the world, with different backgrounds, see different facets of the diamond with greater clarity. It benefits us to learn humbly from our siblings in Christ around the world.

In the context of the historic church, we are able to learn about God from our predecessors in widely different historic and cultural settings than ours. The Holy Spirit has been teaching, nourishing, and guiding the church into truth for the last two thousand years. It has been said that theology should be done with ancient friends. As we engage in theology, we are meant to learn from our brothers and sisters from the early church, from the medieval church, from the Reformation, up until today. When we invite our brothers and sisters from previous centuries into conversation with us, we invite God's wisdom from previous centuries into our lives. We learn that behind our theology lie centuries of both wisdom and foolishness that we can learn from. When we do theology with our ancient friends, we are invited to learn from their wisdom and their mistakes. Doing theology with a historical mindset does not elevate tradition to the same level of authority of Scripture, but rather helps us understand Scripture through the lenses of church history.

Questions We Will Consider in This Book

If you've ever browsed the theology section of a Christian bookstore, you know the truth of the sentiment of Ecclesiastes 12:12: "There is no end to the making of many books." Many of those books are much thicker than the one you currently hold in your hands. That's because it's an introduction, a first step on the journey.

This book will not focus on every theological consideration helpful to the believer. Rather, it will discuss primary topics—the things Christians hold general agreement on. We call these topics *essentials*, or *first-tier doctrines*. They are the defining beliefs of Christianity, the core beliefs that distinguish Christianity from other belief systems and that mark the boundaries between orthodoxy and heresy. If you are familiar with the historic creeds of the church, you will not be surprised to see that this book follows the same pattern.

In an age marked by ignorance of essentials and division over nonessentials, we want to help you retrieve the doctrines that distinguish Christianity and that have done so for two thousand years.

The topics that we will address in this book will be phrased in the form of questions:

- Who is God? *The Doctrine of the Trinity*
- What is God like? *The Attributes of God*
- What is the Bible? *The Doctrine of Scripture*
- Who are we? *The Doctrine of Humanity*
- What went wrong? *The Doctrine of Sin*
- What has God done? *The Doctrines of Christology, Atonement, and Justification*
- To whom do we belong? *The Doctrine of the Church*
- How does the story end? *The Doctrine of Last Things*

Let's get started!

CHAPTER 2

Who Is God?

The Doctrine of the Trinity

Brief Definition: *God eternally exists as one essence and three distinct persons: God the Father, God the Son, and God the Holy Spirit. Each person is fully God, yet there is one God.*

What do you love?

It's one of the most important questions you will ever seek to answer. Think about it: What do you desire? What do you have affection for? What are you drawn toward?

Perhaps a million answers spring to mind. Our application of the word *love* is so broad that we might honestly answer with a list of some length. We love our family—our parents, siblings, grandparents, spouse, kids. We love our hobbies—playing a favorite sport, creating art, listening to soul-stirring music. We love pets. We love houseplants. We love ice cream and salsa. We love experiences like a day at the beach or a hike in the Rockies. But what if you had to answer the question, "What do you love?" with only one response? Could you narrow it down to one thing? Would it be possible for you to say, "I love this one thing more than anything else"?

You may understandably feel hesitant to answer the question. Or you may understandably feel tempted to answer it the way you are "supposed to." Revealing questions should give us pause before we respond. They require something of us. But this particular revealing question is one you are in some sense answering every single moment of every day. You answer it by what you give your time to, what you buy, what you watch. You answer it by what stirs anxiety or joy in you, by what excites or disappoints you. You answer it by what you are looking forward to and what you regret. By who you associate with and whom you admire. Even if you cannot articulate the words, you are answering this question every day by what you give your life to.

In the Gospel of Matthew, a lawyer poses a revealing question to Jesus. Unlike the question we have posed to you, this one is meant to trap. The lawyer asks Him, "Teacher, which is the greatest commandment in the Law?" (Matt. 22:36 ESV).

At first blush, the lawyer's revealing question appears completely unrelated to ours. What does law have to do with love? But it, too, is a question that asks, "What do you love?" The lawyer is, in theory and in practice, someone who loves the law. He and his fellow lawyers, the Pharisees, want to expose Jesus as someone who does not. In the mind of the Pharisee, love of the law answers the question of what is most important, of what is best for humanity, of what God wants most from us. What do you love most? The law of the Lord.

But Jesus takes the premise of his revealing question and reframes it:

> "You shall *love* the Lord your God with all your
> heart and with all your soul and with all your
> mind. This is the great and first command-
> ment. And a second is like it: You shall *love* your
> neighbor as yourself. On these two command-
> ments depend all the Law and the Prophets."
> (Matt. 22:37–40 ESV, emphasis added)

He then tells a parable about a man beaten and left for dead on the road to Jericho. It is a story in which the religious figures exhibit perfect obedience to the ritual laws and colossal failure to the law of Love. Jesus understands that life is ultimately a contest of loves. As His interactions with the Pharisees will consistently reveal, it is possible to love a good thing in place of a better thing. It is possible to love a shadow in place of its fulfillment. Incredibly, it is possible to love what God has said without loving God Himself or those made in His image.

The Pharisee counts himself as an exemplary disciple based on what he knows. Jesus reframes the concept of discipleship through the lens of what we love. Or, more precisely, whom we love.

So, whom do you love? Whom do you love more than anything else?

You know the right answer. But as we begin our study of theology, we want you to be able to give that answer from a place of having meditated on why it is the right one. The true one. The beautiful one. The best one. We want you to love giving the answer because you love the "who" it speaks of. That "who" is the starting point for all theological insight.

What are the consequences if we don't get the doctrine of God right? Doctrinal error in any category is serious, but none is more serious than when it comes to the nature and character of God. Our understanding of God is what shapes everything about us. But what happens if we think about God wrongly?

If we willingly believe things about God that are not true, we are charting a dangerous course. We are telling God who He is supposed to be. When we relegate Trinitarianism to irrelevancy, we risk following the pattern of virtually every major heretical view of God over the last two thousand years. Maybe most importantly, if we get the doctrine of God wrong, we will likely get every other doctrine wrong because every other Christian belief finds its beginning in the doctrine of God. Most doctrines are like limbs on a tree—firm limbs—but limbs, nonetheless. The doctrine of God is the trunk, and no limb can live without the trunk.

If we get the doctrine of God wrong, we face very real consequences in our daily lives. Conceive of Him as able to be controlled? Watch your prayers turn into negotiation sessions and your moral behaviors turn to efforts to earn His favor. Conceive of Him as gracious and loving, but not just? Watch your sin grab a stranglehold as you assure yourself, "He'll forgive me!" Think He isn't all-seeing? Prepare for the illusion of secret sins to pounce and devour you. Think He withholds good things from His children? The way you spend your time and money will show the signs. The way you love your neighbor will carry the marks. Any small or skewed conception of who God is breaks the second commandment: it forms Him into an idol. And idols are cruel taskmasters.

In this chapter and the next, we will examine the "who" of theology in the doctrine of God. We will begin with a discussion of His Trinity, and then we will explore His attributes (what is true of His nature). Because these chapters concern a "who," read them expectantly, looking for how they are both intensely personal and intensely practical in their application.

God Is Triune

Let's start with a little honesty. Think back over your relationship with the Bible. Think of your favorite passages you return to again and again. Think of your favorite insights, the moments that moved you to tears, the verses you wrote on note cards to memorize because of their necessity and beauty. How many of them centered on the Trinity of God? Outside of singing the hymn "Holy, Holy, Holy," most of us are not likely to have attached feelings of warmth or gratitude to the idea that God eternally exists as one essence and three distinct persons. It's a doctrine rarely taught and even more rarely meditated upon. Yet, it forms an essential belief of Christianity.

Though it is rarely taught today, it has not always been so. The Apostles' Creed, the Nicene Creed, and the Athanasian Creed are all built upon it, words repeated Sunday after Sunday for centuries—by believers new and old, learned and unlearned—so important were their truths to the training up of disciples. Important and beautiful. And practical. Trinitarianism is not a doctrine only for elite systematic theologians or for pastors deeply immersed in study. It is for every level of theologian. It is for you.

Admittedly, of all the doctrines we will examine, this one can be the most intimidating. To make progress in our understanding of Trinitarianism, we will need to hold in tension two important instincts: oneness and threeness. Both are essential. Lose one of them and we lose orthodoxy. If God is only one, we lose the distinct persons of the Father, Son, and Spirit. If God is three, we lose the beautiful unity of the one God. Heresy seeks to relieve the tension that the Bible demands. Orthodoxy requires us to hold that tension. God is one and three.

There Is One God

The first instinct of Trinitarianism is the belief in one God. The Bible does not advocate belief in three Gods, or numerous gods, but one. He is the Lord, the Creator of all things.

The Bible begins with the claim, "In the beginning God created the heavens and the earth" (Gen. 1:1). Do not miss the significance of that first sentence. The Bible begins with a stunning claim: there is one God.

Imagine how this statement would have landed on the ears of its original audience, Israel, waiting in the wilderness between Egypt and Canaan. For four hundred years, they had lived in a polytheistic land, the fruit of their labors pulled from their hands to be offered up to a pantheon of Egyptian gods. Here they stood, poised to enter into a land with a pantheon of equal size. The Canaanite gods were equally numerous, and equally demanding. And God declares there is no pantheon at all, but a mono-theon. It is a message embedded in the covenant He had declared to Abraham, Isaac, and Jacob, and it is a message He had declared to Moses at the burning bush: "I AM WHO I AM" (Exod. 3:14). The so-called gods of Egypt and Canaan might claim, "I am the god of rain or harvest or childbirth," but none could make this claim. Only the God of the Bible can say: "I AM."

In the wilderness wandering, Israel finds comfort in God's oneness: "Listen, Israel, the LORD our God, the LORD is one" (Deut. 6:4). They owe all of their allegiance to Him and Him alone. Similarly, our worship cannot be divided. We worship the God who creates all things and redeems us from slavery to sin, and we worship Him alone. Just as Israel would run to foreign gods, we, too, are tempted to trade our mono-theon for a pantheon. Like them, we need to hear, again and again, that the Lord our God is one.

God's oneness remained in the hearts and on the lips of Israel's faithful all the way into New Testament times. This is what makes Jesus's claim in John 10:10 so bold. He says, "I and the Father are one" (John 10:30). We will explore Jesus's claim of unity and equality with God in chapter 7, but note here that He reiterates the historic claim that there is only one God. The gods of Babylon, Persia, Greece, and Rome are not gods at all. According to Jesus, there is only one God.

The New Testament authors preserve this teaching, as well. Paul reminds the church in Galatia, full of Jewish and Gentile believers, that "God is one" (Gal. 3:20). Over and over again, the Bible asserts there is only one God who is Creator, Sustainer, and providential Ruler over all things.

As in the days of Abraham and Moses, as in the days of Jesus and Paul, so in every era of human history we have been drawn to belief in many gods. Or in no god at all. The Bible emphatically disagrees. There is one God, and He alone is worthy of worship.

The oneness of God is the first of two important instincts for Trinitarianism. It is what distinguishes the God of the Bible from the many gods and godlessness of human invention.

God Is Three Persons

The second important instinct for Trinitarianism is the threeness. God is one God, but He is One God who *eternally* exists as three distinct persons—the Father, the Son, and the Spirit. Each person is fully God. But the Father is not the Son, and the Holy Spirit is not the Father or the Son, but they are the triune God who is perfectly one and distinct in three persons. The threeness of God is not a form of polytheism because Christians worship just one God. Nor would Christianity teach particular or preferential worship of any of the three persons within the godhead.

Confused yet? Let's break it down by asking a few further questions: What distinguishes each person of the Trinity? What makes the Father, Father? What makes the Son, Son? And what makes the Spirit, Spirit?

If ever an analogy offered help, it would seem that now would be the time to employ one. Maybe you have heard some analogies for the Trinity: God is an egg: a shell, white, and a yolk. God is like water: ice, water, and steam. God is like a three-leaf clover. Though at first these honorable attempts may seem helpful, they can actually hinder our understanding of the diversity of the three persons in the Godhead. Fortunately, the Bible offers some simple language that helps us with distinguishing the three persons.

Two categories that have historically helped Christians see the distinctions of each person are the Immanent Trinity and the Economic Trinity. The Immanent Trinity refers to God in Himself—even before creation. The *Economic Trinity* refers to how we see the *Immanent Trinity* revealed in redemptive history. What we see in Scripture is that:

Economic Trinity

God the Father initiates the plan for salvation.

God the Son accomplishes salvation.

God the Spirit applies salvation.

Immanent Trinity

The Father, eternally unbegotten.

The Son, eternally begotten by the Father.

The Spirit, eternally proceeds from the Father and the Son.

In order to see these two categories more clearly, we give our attention to how the Bible describes each person and what they do. To understand what distinguishes each person, we look to what each person does in the biblical story. What do we know of each person as it relates to their redemptive acts in history that give us insight into their eternal relations as Father, Son, and Spirit? Here are the three keys:

1. God the Father is never sent in Scripture. That means He is eternally unsent or eternally unbegotten. Who is God the Father? The eternally unsent.

2. God the Son is sent by the Father in Scripture. That means He is eternally sent or eternally begotten. Who is God the Son? The eternally sent by the Father.

3. God the Holy Spirit is sent by the Father and the Son in Scripture. That means He eternally proceeds from the Father and the Son. Who is God the Spirit? The eternally sent by the Father and Son.

Let's explore further into each person's unique role in redemptive history.

God the Father

What does it mean—and why does it matter—that God the Father is eternally unsent? The Bible reveals that God the Father, the first person of the Trinity, is the source of all divine activity. At no time in the biblical story is the Father sent. Consider John 3:16 (ESV), "For God so loved the world, that he gave his only Son, that whoever believes in him should not perish but have eternal life." In His love for the world, the Father sent His only Son.

Every divine action starts with the Father. Jesus says, "Truly I tell you, the Son is not able to do anything on his own, but only what he sees the Father doing. For whatever the Father does, the Son likewise does these things. For the Father loves the Son and shows him everything he is doing, and he will show him greater works than these so that you will be amazed" (John 5:19–20). The Father initiates everything.

The unique eternal characteristic of God the Father is His Fatherhood, or that He is eternally unsent. This is a profound insight because it means that before God was the Creator, He is eternally a Father—a Father to the Son. There has never been a time when God the Father was not a Father. He has always been a Father to the Son.

It's understandable that, for some of us, our earthly fathers have tainted our understanding of what a father is and what a father does. The idea of the fatherhood of God may not seem like good news. But what if, instead of looking at God the Father through the lens of our earthly fathers, we looked at our earthly fathers through the lens of our perfect Father in heaven? We have a heavenly Father who gives light and life to all of His children. As John reminds us, "This is the message we have heard from him and declare to you: God is light, and there is absolutely no darkness in him" (1 John 1:5). Though we have imperfect earthly fathers, we have a perfect Father in heaven. Good news.

God the Son

If the unique act of the Father is that He is never sent, which makes Him eternally unbegotten, what distinguishes the Son from the Father and the Spirit?

The Son is eternally sent from the Father (cf. John 3:16). The Son is not subordinate to the Father, but He is sent by Him. The Bible teaches the equality of the Son with the Father and the sending of the Son in the opening verses of John's Gospel. In John 1:1 we are told that the Son is God: "In the beginning was the Word, and the Word was with God, and the Word was God." The Son of God, the Word, has eternally existed with God. But a few verses later, John also tells us that the Word was sent and that He assumed upon Himself a human nature by tabernacling among us (John 1:14).

How can this happen? Because, "for just as the Father has life in himself, so also he has granted to the Son to have life in himself" (John 5:26). The Father has life in Himself. And the Father eternally grants not just that the Son has life but life in Himself. This distinguishes the Father from the Son, yet they are also one (John 10:30).

Paul, too, highlights the distinct person of the Son:

> He is the image of the invisible God, the firstborn of all creation. For by him all things were created, in heaven and on earth, visible and invisible, whether thrones or dominions or rulers or authorities—all things were created through him and for him. And he is before all things, and in him all things hold together. And he is the head of the body, the church. He is the beginning, the firstborn from the dead, that in everything he might be preeminent. For in him all the fullness of God was pleased to dwell, and through him to reconcile to himself all things, whether on earth or in heaven, making peace by the blood of his cross. (Col. 1:15–20 ESV)

Here, Paul rightly holds the tension between oneness and threeness. He tells us the Son is the "image of the invisible God." That means He was sent by the Father to represent what God is like to us. The Son, Jesus, is God. Paul includes the Son in the act of creation and even claims that He is the goal of all of creation. All things were created *through* Him and *for* Him.

Not only does the Son share with His Father in the creation of all things, but uniquely, He reconciles to Himself all things. How? By being sent from the Father to make peace through the blood of His cross. The Father is not sent to the cross; only the Son is sent to the cross. Since the Father is unsent in history, only the Son is able to reconcile all things because He was sent by the Father. The Father sends; the Son is sent.

The sending of the Son is central to our understanding of the gospel. The triune God has so set His affection upon you that God the Father sent God the Son to die on the cross on your behalf.

God the Spirit

The Father is unsent. The Son is sent by the Father. What distinguishes the Spirit from the Father and the Son? The Spirit is sent by the Father *and* the Son.

The Bible teaches that the Holy Spirit is God Himself by ascribing divine activities and attributes to Him. He has the name of God ascribed to Him (Acts 5:3–4), He participates in creation (Gen. 1:2), He is everywhere present (Ps. 139:7),

He is all knowing (1 Cor. 2:10), and He is all-powerful (Ps. 33:6). The Holy Spirit shares in the same essence as the Father and the Son. He is God, and there is only one God.

But the Holy Spirit's activity in redemptive history distinguishes Him from the Father and the Son. Describing the person and work of the Holy Spirit, Jesus tells His disciples, "But when the Helper comes, whom I will send to you from the Father, the Spirit of truth, who proceeds from the Father, he will bear witness about me. And you also will bear witness, because you have been with me from the beginning" (John 15:26–27 ESV). Jesus says that the unique act of the Spirit in redemption is to be sent by the Father *and* the Son. Some theologians have called this the procession of the Spirit. He proceeds from both the Father and the Son. His mission is to indwell the church and to bear witness about the Son.

Why the Trinity Is Good News

Let's review what we have learned:

The Immanent Trinity	The Economic Trinity
The Father is eternally unbegotten.	The Father initiates and sends.
The Son is eternally begotten.	The Son is sent and accomplishes.
The Spirit eternally proceeds from the Father and Son.	The Spirit proceeds and applies.

So, what does all this mean? Consider a few practical and beautiful implications of God the Trinity.

First, God is one. There is only one God, and He alone is worthy of worship. Think how many times this week, today, this hour, or maybe even this minute you have set your affections on a multitude of lesser things. The pleasures and distractions of this world are vying for our affections and attention in place of God. Our possessions, our work, and our relationships become objects of our worship instead of means for worship of the One who gives them. The oneness of God helps us to direct our worship away from the pantheon of our earthly desires to the only worthy Object of adoration.

Second, the gospel is only possible if God is Trinity. Each member of the Trinity plays an essential role. God the Father initiates. God the Son accomplishes. God the Spirit applies. Only the triune God can love sinners, die for sinners, live with sinners, and make sinners saints.

Finally, the triune God not only forgives sin, He invites us into fellowship with each person of the Godhead. At the heart of the Christian life is a communing fellowship with each person of the Trinity. The fellowship enjoyed between the three Persons for all eternity invites you to partake of its riches.

You are invited to fellowship specifically with God the Father. God the Father declares we are His sons and daughters. He has adopted us. We were once spiritual orphans, but the Father has brought us into His family. God the Father has set His affections upon you, and He will never abandon you. He loves you the same way He loves His Son.

You are invited to fellowship specifically with God the Son. God the Son came to bear your shame and guilt. Because of Him, you no longer stand condemned, but free. Free to be assured of God's love for you. Free to reciprocate that love. He is our brother, our mediator, our king who invites us to be coheirs in His kingdom.

You are invited to fellowship specifically with God the Holy Spirit. You no longer have to go to a temple to experience the presence of God. The Spirit now resides in you. He delights to be with you. In His presence you can know that God delights in you.

So, back to those revealing questions. What is the most important question we will ever seek to answer? As it turns out, it's not, "What do you love?" And it's not even, "Whom do you love?"—though how we answer both of those questions reveals the state of our hearts. The most important question we can ever seek to answer is this:

"Who loves you?"

God does. The one true God, the triune God. Say that answer out loud, no pondering or soul-searching required. Any love we have for God is only because He first loved us (1 John 4:19). The doctrine of the Trinity is the doctrine of God's love. You are loved by God the Father, you are loved by God the Son, and you are loved by God the Holy Spirit.

WHO IS GOD?

Good news. The love of the triune God toward you is the genesis for all other loves and the beginning of a love we will enjoy and explore for all eternity.

You Are a Theologian

Discuss

1. Why do you think the Trinity is so seldom taught, pondered, or celebrated in Christian circles today? What do we lose by neglecting this doctrine?

2. How is the oneness of God a necessary reminder for you personally? What divided worship does it challenge?

3. Of the three persons of the Trinity, which do you feel most acquainted with? Which is easiest to attach your affections and worship to? How does your personal history of family or church shape the answers you gave?

4. What church traditions tend to emphasize one member of the Trinity over others? How is this potentially dangerous for our understanding of how God relates to us in the gospel?

5. On a scale from 1 to 10, rank your comfort level with the doctrine of the Trinity before reading this chapter. Now rank

47

it after reading this chapter. Which insights do you most want to remember? Which insights do you want to explore further?

Pray

Use the outline below to write a prayer to the Father, through the Son, and in the power of the Spirit. Use it to answer the question, "Who loves you?" by acknowledging each person's divinity and each person's delight in you.

Heavenly Father,

Thank You that You love me . . .

Thank You that You sent the Son . . .

Thank You that You, Father, and the Son have sent the Spirit . . .

Though I am _____,
the Father delights in me.

Though I am _____,
the Son delights in me.

Though I am _____,
the Spirit delights in me.

Father, through Your Son and by Your Spirit, teach me to live as if I believe this and to love in return as I have been loved.

Amen.

CHAPTER 3

What Is God Like?

The Attributes of God

Brief Definition: *God is knowable. His nature and character are revealed to us through the Bible. We understand His character traits as both incommunicable (His alone) and communicable (able to become ours).*

One of the most memorable Christmas movies of all time is *Elf*, the story of Buddy, a human raised as an elf at the North Pole, who goes in search of his father in New York City. It will not surprise you that we find the movie to be deeply theological.

After all, who doesn't look to Will Farrell movies for deep theological truth? At one point in the movie, Buddy learns that Santa is scheduled to visit the department store where he works. He exclaims, "Santa??? I KNOW HIM!!!" The next day, a department store Santa reports for work, complete with a fake beard and hokey "Ho Ho Ho." The kids waiting to see him sense nothing amiss, but Buddy loses it: "You're a fake. You sit on a throne of lies." And my favorite: "You don't smell like Santa. You smell like beef and cheese." Before we connect Buddy to the doctrine of God, let's put that relatable elf on the shelf and explore the doctrine itself.

The doctrine of God is the study of His character traits. We call the character traits of God His attributes. God's attributes describe who He is, and they imply how He acts.

When Paul addresses the Athenians on the Areopagus, he remarks on having seen an altar with the inscription, "To the unknown god" (Acts 17:23 ESV). Paul then announces good news of a particular kind: the Christian God is knowable. He is knowable, and He makes Himself known.

The attributes of God are typically organized into two categories: incommunicable and communicable. But these terms themselves can be difficult to understand. When we speak of a disease being communicable, we mean it is able to be transmitted. Similarly, when we speak of incommunicable or communicable attributes of God, we mean those that are transmittable or nontransmittable.

God's incommunicable attributes are only true of God. They cannot be communicated (or transmitted) to humans. They set Him apart from His Creation. God's communicable attributes are true of God but can also become true of us. They can be transmitted to humans. Here is an example of a breakdown of the two categories:

Incommunicable Attributes *Only God is:*	**Communicable Attributes** *God is (and we can be):*
Infinite	Holy
Incomprehensible	Loving
Self-existent	Just
Self-sufficient	Good
Eternal	Merciful
Immutable	Gracious
Omnipresent	Long-suffering
Omniscient	Wise
Omnipotent	Jealous (for His glory)
Sovereign	Wrathful
Transcendent	Faithful
	Righteous
	Truthful

Every trait on both lists is limitlessly true of God. Once the Holy Spirit dwells in us, the list on the right can become true of us. It is a list we grow into as we walk in obedience to the commands of God. When we talk about being "conformed to the image of Christ," this is the list we are describing. It shows us how to *reflect* who God is as Christ did.[4]

Because God is infinite, the number of things that are knowable about Him is also infinite. Though finite human minds can't know an infinite God fully, we can know him sufficiently for life and godliness. He has revealed all we need in scripture (more on this in chapter 4), and we will not have exhausted that revelation in this lifetime.

The two lists above do not even exhaust the attributes disclosed in the Bible, but they make a good start at it. And they can help with Bible reading in an age that tells us the Bible is primarily a tool for self-discovery. By acquainting ourselves with the categories and definitions of God's attributes, we become better at reading the Bible first to see what it says about God and second what it says about (or to) us. The more we learn to read the Bible this way, the more we begin to recognize that what it teaches about Him will more than occupy us during this lifetime. And eternity will grant us limitless opportunity to explore the rest of what we can know about Him, without ever reaching the end of that glorious knowledge.

Here are some brief definitions and Scripture references for our working list of attributes:[5]

Incommunicable Attributes

Infinite: God has no limits or bounds whatsoever in His person or dominion (1 Kings 8:27; Ps. 145:3).

Incomprehensible: Because God is God, He is beyond the understanding of humans. His ways, character, and acts are higher than ours. We only understand as God chooses to reveal Himself, His ways, or His purposes (Job 11:7; Rom. 11:33).

Self-existent: God depends on nothing for His existence beyond Himself. The whole basis of His existence is within Himself. At one time nothing but God Himself existed. He added nothing to Himself by creation (Exod. 3:14; John 5:26).

Self-sufficient: Within Himself, God is able to act, that is, to bring about His will without any assistance. Although He may choose to use assistance, it is His good pleasure, not His need that governs that choice (Ps. 50:7–12; Acts 17:24–25).

Eternal: God has no beginning, and He has no end. He is not confined to the finiteness of time or to man's reckoning of time (Deut. 32:40; Isa. 57:15).

Immutable: God is always the same in His nature, His character, and His will. He never changes, and He can never be made to change (Ps. 102:25–27; Mal. 3:6; Heb. 13:8).

Omniscient: God knows all. He has perfect knowledge of everything that is past, present, and future (Job 37:16; Ps. 139:1–6).

Omnipotent: God possesses all power. He is able to bring about anything He has decided to do—with or without the use of any source beyond Himself (Gen. 18:14; Job 42:2; Jer. 32:27).

Omnipresent: God is present everywhere, in all the universe, at all times, in the totality of His character (Prov. 15:3; Jer. 23:23–24).

Sovereign: God is totally, supremely, and preeminently over all His creation. There is not a person or thing that has escaped His control and foreknown plan (Dan. 4:35; Isa. 14:24, 27; Dan. 2:20–23).

Transcendent: God is above His creation, and He would exist if there were no creation. His existence is totally apart from His creatures or creation (Isa. 43:10; Isa. 55:8–9).

Communicable Attributes

Holy: God is a morally excellent, perfect being. He is totally other than man. He is purity of being in every aspect (Lev. 19:2; Job 34:10; Isa. 47:4).

Loving: God's love moves Him to give Himself for another, even to lay down His own life. His love causes Him to desire His creatures' highest good. This love is not based on the worth, response, or merit of the object being loved (Jer. 31:3; Rom. 5:8; 1 John 4:8).

Just: God is fair in all of His actions. Whether He deals with man, angels, or demons, He acts in total equity by rewarding righteousness and punishing sin. Since He knows all, every decree is absolutely just (Num. 14:8; 23:19; Ps. 89:14).

Good: In His goodness God gives to others, not according to what they deserve but according to His good will and kindness toward them (2 Chron. 5:13; Ps. 106:1).

Merciful: God is an actively compassionate being. He responds compassionately toward those who have opposed His will in their pursuit of their own way (Pss. 62:12; 89:14; 106:44–45; 116:5; Rom. 9:14–15).

Gracious: God demonstrates unmerited favor toward His creation. His common grace is shown toward everything He has made, and His special grace is shown toward those who receive salvation through Christ (Ps. 116:5–9; Eph. 1:3–10; 2 Cor. 9:8; Titus 2:11–14).

Long-suffering: God's righteous anger is slow to be kindled against those who fail to listen to His warnings or to obey His instructions. His eternal longing for highest good for His creatures holds back His holy justice (Num. 14:18; 2 Pet. 3:9).

Wise: God's actions are based on His character. His wisdom causes Him to choose righteous ends and to make the most fitting plans to achieve those ends (Isa. 40:28; Dan. 2:20).

Jealous: God is unwilling to share what is rightfully and morally His with any other creature (Exod. 20:5; 34:14).

Wrathful: There is within God a hatred for all that is unrighteous and an unquenchable desire to punish all unrighteousness. Whatever is inconsistent with His holy standard must ultimately be consumed (Exod. 34:6–7; 1 Chron. 19:2; Rom. 1:18).

Faithful: God is always true to His promises. He can never draw back from His promises of blessing or judgment. Since He cannot lie, He is totally steadfast to what He has spoken (Deut. 7:9; 2 Tim. 2:13).

Righteous: God is always good. It is essential to His character. He always does the right thing. Ultimately, since He is God, whatever He does is right. He is the absolute. His actions are always consistent with His character, which is love (Deut. 32:4; Ps. 119:142).

Truthful: All that God says is reality. Whether believed by man or not, whether seen as reality or not, what God has spoken is reality. Whatever He speaks is truth (Num. 23:19; Ps. 31:5; Titus 1:2).

Why a Knowable God Is Good News

So, how does Buddy the Elf declaring Department Store Santa a fraud help us understand the doctrine of God as good news?

Buddy knows a fake Santa because Buddy knows the real Santa. He knows him firsthand. And this is the gift we receive as those with a knowable God: we can discern the truth from a fake. The Bible gives us the knowledge of God, but it does this not just so that we can know Him. It does this so that we can worship Him as He deserves. Like Buddy the Elf, we know that only One belongs on the throne. When we devote ourselves to the knowledge of God disclosed to us in His Word, we learn to recognize Him rightly and to offer Him right worship.

But we also gain something else: we learn how to adore Him rightly. Buddy doesn't just know Santa, he doesn't just revere Santa, he loves him. He loves and values him accurately because he knows him well. His knowledge shapes his affection. The same is true for us. The more we grow in our knowledge of God, the more we grow in our love for Him. We perceive with ever-increasing depth His value and worth as an object of our adoration. We become less and less capable of being fooled by or satisfied with a substitute. We also become less and less prone to *creating* a substitute, whittling

God into our own image by choosing only some of His attributes to celebrate and ignoring or downplaying others.

And we gain yet another gift in our knowing of God: the ability to understand ourselves in relation to Him. Buddy doesn't just know Santa; he knows the difference between Santa and his elves. As the seventeenth-century theologian John Calvin famously noted, "The knowledge of God and the knowledge of self always go hand in hand. There is no true knowledge of self apart from the knowledge of God. The doctrine of God shows us the distance between a transcendent God and His created image-bearers, and it simultaneously draws us toward imitation."[6]

He is wonderfully unlike and like us. We need both of these perspectives to bear His image as we were created to do. We cannot conform to the image of a God we do not know, nor can we worship Him as we were created. In knowing Him, we know ourselves and our fellow humans rightly. Our identity is derivative of His.

The more we learn of Him, the more we love Him. The more we learn of Him, the more we love ourselves and our neighbors as we ought. And the more we want to proclaim to everyone we meet: "I know Him!!!"

You Are a Theologian

Discuss

1. Which of God's attributes are you most familiar with? Which are less familiar to you? Why?

2. Which of God's attributes make you feel uncomfortable? Which feel most relatable or understandable? Why?

3. Choose one incommunicable attribute and discuss how it increases your understanding of your own limits. How does it increase your love for God? How does it enliven you to worship?

4. Choose one communicable attribute and discuss how it increases your understanding of your own limits. How does it increase your love for God? How does it enliven you to worship?

Pray

1. Choose three incommunicable attributes of God and write a prayer of thanksgiving and praise.

2. Choose three communicable attributes of God and write a prayer of request that He would make you more like Christ in these ways.

CHAPTER 4

What Is the Bible?

Revelation: The Doctrine of Scripture

Brief Definition: *God can be truly known. He graciously makes Himself known to us through Scripture. The Bible is inspired, authoritative, inerrant, infallible, necessary, sufficient, and clear.*

One of our friends is an avid movie buff. He recently watched *The Sixth Sense* for the first time. As soon as the movie was over, he texted us in complete shock (spoiler alert): "You're telling me he was dead the whole time???" How our friend had managed to avoid learning the shocking plot twist of a movie released thirty years ago defies explanation. Yet here he was, having that same moment so many others have had, realizing everything he had thought was true had actually turned out to be false.

Hollywood knows how much we are pulled toward movies that pose the question, *How do we know what we know?* Other blockbusters like *The Matrix, The Illusionist,* and *Inception* bear witness to our fascination with how we know what we know. How can I be confident that what I see, hear, or experience is real? Am I easily deceived? Does my perception of reality actually align with reality? And these questions are by no means new. Humans have always asked them: philosophers and children, rich and poor, educated and uneducated, ancient and modern, Christians and unbelievers.

And theologians.

When theologians ask, "How do we know what we know?" they do so with the knowledge of God in view. As it relates to theology, the essential questions that emerge are: *Is God knowable? If so, how can I know Him? And how can I be confident that I actually know Him?*

Some belief systems conclude that God is unknowable. Others conclude that knowledge of God may be discovered through pure human effort or by secret knowledge revealed to the individual. But Christianity makes the astonishing claim that God can indeed be known and that we know Him only because He has made Himself known. Under no obligation to do so, in His unmatched grace and goodness, He has disclosed Himself to us. His purpose in doing so is relational: so that we can know and love Him. Theologians call the study of God's disclosure of Himself the doctrine of revelation.

Don't miss this distinction: Christianity distinguishes all knowledge of God as revealed knowledge. We do not discover God. We don't stumble across Him or search Him out, but rather, He makes Himself known. He reveals Himself to us. We cannot know God unless He gives Himself to us in revelation. Because of the effects of sin, we are born without knowledge of God, rendering us spiritually deaf and blind. It is not through our own efforts, but only through His mercy that we can know Him. And in His great mercy, He gives us ears to hear and eyes to see!

To the question "Is God knowable?," Christianity answers, "Yes. He makes Himself known through divine revelation."

Because God is the actor in revealing Himself, because only He can give sight to the spiritually blind, we understand the entire task of theology as one done in humility. All other fields of knowledge investigate, dissect, and hypothesize. They initiate the task of discovery. In theology we certainly study, work, and explore, but we do so in response to having received God's disclosure of Himself. Theologians receive the revelation God gives to us.

As I (Jen) write, I am listening to a favorite piece of classical music. When I first heard it several decades ago, I had not gone searching for it. Rather, it found me. I was invited to a performance where I was introduced to it and found the experience of hearing it to be, well, revelatory. In the intervening years, I have made meditation on this particular piece, listening to it many times, savoring its heights and depths, discerning its different instruments, learning about its composer and the reason for which it was composed. I received the knowledge of it, and having ears to hear, have since explored and analyzed it. And the result has been increasing enjoyment and appreciation of its beauty.

Our God reveals Himself to us, and we respond to His clearly perceived beauty by devoting ourselves to that revelation, and our joy and affection for Him grow. Or, at least, that's how it should go. But more on that in a bit. Having asserted that God can be known because He makes Himself known, the next questions are: *How* does He make Himself known? Where do we look for knowledge of God?

God's revelation of Himself falls into two categories: general revelation and special revelation.

General Revelation

"The heavens declare the glory of God, and the sky above proclaims his handiwork. Day to day pours out speech, and night to night reveals knowledge" (Ps. 19:1–2 ESV). These words of the psalmist summarize what theologians call *general revelation*. Put simply, God makes Himself known in what He makes. Anytime you gaze on a sunset, anytime you inhale the scent of spring blossoms, anytime you marvel at a snow-capped mountain or the blazing colors of fall, you are not just witnessing the beauty of God's creation; you are witnessing a testimony to God's existence and nature. Creation is glorifying and revealing its Creator. God makes Himself known in what He has made.

Paul gives us a similar idea when he teaches us,

> For the wrath of God is revealed from heaven against all ungodliness and unrighteousness of men, who by their unrighteousness suppress the truth. For what can be known about God is plain to them, because God has shown it to them. For his invisible attributes, namely, his eternal power and divine nature, have been clearly perceived, ever since the creation of the world, in the things that have been made. So they are without excuse. (Rom. 1:18–20 ESV)

Paul tells us that God's invisible attributes, His power, His nature, can be clearly perceived in the creation of the world. But He also tells us that our natural response is to suppress the truth of God in His creation. God's revelation through creation is of a general nature because, while it declares that He exists, it does not proclaim the way of salvation. It is a partial disclosure, sufficient to establish our guilt when we do not offer God worship, but it is insufficient to save. It is also general because it is directed to a general audience—all humans. We don't fully come to know God through general revelation. But the problem lies not with general revelation; it lies with the nature of humanity. We take the things God has created and worship them as though they were the Creator. We worship the *made* and not the *Maker*.

Paul continues, "Claiming to be wise, they became fools, and exchanged the glory of the immortal God for images resembling mortal man and birds and animals and creeping things" (Rom. 1:22–23 ESV). We can know God through His creation, but that knowledge does not redeem us; rather, it condemns us. Creation gives us a knowledge of God as Creator, but we need to know God as Redeemer. We need a knowledge that gives new life. We call that knowledge *special revelation*.

Special Revelation

While all humans receive general revelation of God through His creation, only some receive special revelation. It is "special" in the sense that it has a specific audience (believers) and a specific purpose (salvation). God reveals knowledge sufficient for salvation in Christ and in the Scriptures.

Christ

Jesus came to accomplish salvation, and He did exactly that. But that is not all He accomplished. He also came to make God known to us. Jesus shows us exactly what God is like. He is "the image of the invisible God" (Col. 1:15). He is the exact imprint of the nature and character of God.

When we come to know who Jesus is, we come to know who God is. Jesus shows us exactly what God is like. Jesus is the true image, the perfect reflection, the exact representation of God.

The author of Hebrews claims, "Long ago, at many times and in many ways, God spoke to our fathers by the prophets, but in these last days he has spoken to us by his Son, whom he appointed the heir of all things, through whom also he created the world. He is the radiance of the glory of God and the exact imprint of his nature" (Heb. 1:1–3 ESV). When we encounter Jesus, we are truly encountering God. (More on this in a future chapter.)

It can be easy to think of God in one way and Jesus in another. Our view of God may be of an old man in the sky, gazing judgmentally with a furrowed brow, while our view of Jesus is one of gentle compassion and tenderness. But if we hold a distinction between what God is like and what Jesus is like, we have not properly understood God's revelation to us in Christ. If our understanding of God is not consistent with "the exact imprint of his nature," we likely don't have in view a God to be worshipped but an idol to be killed. God is *Jesus*.

Not only that, but God cannot be truly known apart from Jesus. We may be able to surmise some facts about God from general revelation—that He exists, that He is powerful, that He is creative. But we can't *personally* know God except through Jesus. Jesus is not *a* revelation of God; He is *the* revelation of God.

God is not knowable apart from Jesus, but God is known perfectly in Jesus. If we know Jesus, we know God. But here we are, two thousand years removed from Jesus's earthly ministry. He no longer walks among us but is reigning and ruling in heaven. So, how do we come to a deeper and more intimate knowledge of Him? Through the special revelation given to us in the Bible. The Bible reveals Christ to us.

What Is the Bible?

Taken at face value, the Bible is a collection of sixty-six books written across approximately fifteen hundred years, by more than forty different authors. The fact that its message is consistent and has withstood the test of time is evidence of its miraculous origins and nature. We turn our attention now to the doctrine of Scripture, which gives us seven categories for the Bible's miraculous origin and nature, as well as its purpose. It asserts that the Bible is inspired, authoritative, inerrant, infallible, clear, necessary, and sufficient.

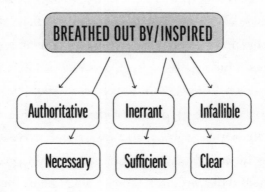

1. Inspired: The Bible, God's Speech

When we speak of the doctrine of inspiration, we do not mean the typical understanding of the word. The Bible is not inspired in the same way that a Rembrandt painting is. It is not merely the product of a moment of great insight. The apostle Paul tells us, "All Scripture is *inspired by God* and is profitable for teaching, for rebuking, for correcting, for training in righteousness, so that the man of God may be complete, equipped for every good work" (2 Tim. 3:16–17, emphasis added). This is one of the most important verses *in* the Bible *about* the Bible. The term that is translated "inspired" is *theopneustos*, or "breathed out by God." It is itself a breathtaking claim. We must not underestimate the importance of what Paul is telling us. Paul is claiming that the Bible is God's Word, His speech, His very breath.

To put it simply, there is an unbelievably close relationship between God and His Word.

Similarly, the apostle Peter claims, "We also have the prophetic word strongly confirmed, and you will do well to pay attention to it, as to a lamp shining in a dark place, until the day dawns and the morning star rises in your hearts. Above all, you know this: No prophecy of Scripture comes from the prophet's own interpretation, because no prophecy ever came by the will of man; instead, men spoke from God as they were carried along by the Holy Spirit" (2 Pet. 1:19–21). This means that all sixty-six books of the Bible are truly the Word of God, fundamentally different from any other text.

The doctrine of inspiration maintains that the original manuscripts are the very words of God, that all parts of Scripture are equally inspired, and that every text also was written by a human author. Put simply, *every biblical text has two authors: a human author and the divine Author. It is both human and divine.*

Every text has a human author. God could have transmitted His words to us through any medium. But He chose to do so through human authors putting words on a page. Human authorship means we should expect Paul to use language differently from John, and Moses to write differently than Jeremiah. Their personalities, viewpoints, and context are on full display. The Bible is a fully human document.

Yet, unlike other human documents, the Bible is without error. That's because every text is also authored by the triune God. The human authors, as Peter just reminded us, wrote as they were "carried along by the Holy Spirit." The Bible, from beginning to end, is the very Word of God.

The doctrine of inspiration is *the* key doctrine for understanding what the Bible is. Everything we can say about what the Bible is flows from our understanding of inspiration. The Bible is the very breath, the very voice of God. Since the Bible is written by God, it begins to take on some of the characteristics of the author. With inspiration fully in view, we can now examine the six other attributes of Scripture, as they flow logically from the assertion that God is the origin of the words we call the Bible.

2. Authoritative: The Bible, Our Good Governor

The Bible, having God as its divine Author, shares in God's authority. It has the right to govern us in all matters of faith and conduct, and it holds the final authority on life and godliness. When God speaks, He always speaks with authority. The Bible is *authoritative* because God is authoritative. To discount the authority of Scripture in any area is to not only discount not only the Bible but the authority of God Himself. The Bible carries with it the same authority as the triune God.

The Bible's authority is regularly an object of intense scrutiny and questioning. Human sinfulness, since Genesis 3, has led us to ask the question: "Did God really say . . . ? The authority of Scripture is not something to be challenged but embraced. The authority of Scripture is profoundly for our good. It is the voice of a loving father tenderly guiding His children into the good life. Scripture's authority leads us into life.

Because the Bible carries the authority of its divine Author, to disobey or disbelieve God's Word is to disobey and disbelieve God. To obey and trust God's Word is to obey and trust God.

3. Inerrant: The Bible, Free from Error

Because its Author is perfect, the Bible is also perfect, or without error. The doctrine of inerrancy asserts that the Bible contains no errors is in all that it affirms and teaches. God's Word is truthful in every respect, even as Jesus affirms, "Your word is truth" (John 17:17). The Bible is a product of the ministry of the Holy Spirit, and the Holy Spirit is "the Spirit of truth" (John 14:17). John also teaches us that "God is light, and in him is no darkness at all" (1 John 1:5 ESV). God cannot lie and He cannot deceive. God the Father's Word is perfect and true. God the Son's Word is perfect and true. God the Spirit's Word is perfect and true.

Though the Bible is inerrant, our interpretation of it may not be. In fact, we may err in interpretation with regularity if we do not understand or apply sound rules of interpretation. Nevertheless, the error lies with human effort, not with divine speech.

4. Infallible: The Bible, God's Unfailing Word

Inerrancy affirms the Bible is free of error. Infallibility affirms the Bible can be trusted. Because the Bible is God's words, it is infallible (or unfailing) in what it says. Luke 1:37 (NIV) tells us that "no word from God will ever fail." Put another way, the Bible can be trusted. As J. I Packer says, Scripture is trustworthy "as a guide that is not deceived and does not deceive."[7] What the Bible calls good is good, and what it calls evil is evil. What it promises can be trusted. What it relates of history actually transpired. What it predicts will come to pass.

Psalm 33:4 tells us, "For the word of the LORD is right, and all his work is trustworthy." In a world filled with lying liars, God's Word speaks only and always in integrity. It is credible in what it says. It can bear our trust because its Author is trustworthy and true.

5. *Necessary: The Bible, God's Good Provision*

Though general revelation gives us knowledge that God exists, in the Bible we are given revelation necessary for salvation, sanctification, and relationship with God. Something that is necessary is needful, indispensable, required, essential. The Bible is all of these things to us.

The Bible is necessary for our salvation because it gives us the story of redemption that culminates in Christ, by whom we are saved. The Bible is necessary for our sanctification because it shows us how those who are saved in Christ should live, making known to us the path of life (Ps. 16:11).

In the Bible we are given revelation necessary for knowing God, specifically for the purpose of relationship with Him. It is the place we go to know God on earth. Without the Bible we would be in complete darkness about who God is, who we are, what Christ accomplished, and the joy of salvation. The Bible is necessary for life and godliness.

6. *Sufficient: The Bible, God's Complete Provision*

Not only does the Bible provide what is necessary for life and godliness, but it does so sufficiently. It is not a revelation that needs to be added to. In it we have all we need in order to know Christ and follow Him. That is not to say that God does not have an ongoing relationship of communication and communion with us through the Holy Spirit. He does. But it is to say that in Scripture we find provision sufficient to see us through this life.

The Bible gives everything we need to be equipped to live a life that is fully pleasing to God. If we want to follow God, if we truly desire to know Him and follow Him, doing so begins with an intimate knowledge of Scripture. It is the means by which the Spirit applies truth to our lives. The Holy Spirit equips us with God's Word, and He equips us to know God's Word.

7. Clear: God's Understandable Message

Anyone who has ever read the book of Revelation may hesitate at our final attribute of Scripture. The Bible is given to us in clarity. It has been written in such a way that it can be understood by God's people. God has given us an intelligible revelation.

Regardless of our gender, age, experience, education, or cultural background, the Holy Spirit has breathed out the Bible for everyone. You don't need to be an academic to understand it. You don't need to have a degree in order to read the Bible. You don't even need to know Greek or Hebrew to understand it. The Bible is meant to clearly reveal God.

This does not mean that all texts are equally easy to understand or that it is easy to understand the Bible as a whole. But where lack of clarity is experienced, the deficiency lies with us, not God's Word. As with all areas of the Christian life, gaining a clear understanding of the Bible requires discipline and the use of good tools on the part of the learner. We do our best to present ourselves to God "as one approved, a worker who does not need to be ashamed and who correctly handles the word of truth" (2 Tim. 2:15 NIV). We grow in our appreciation of the Bible's clarity as we grow in our ability to read it diligently.

What Does the Bible Do?

Now that we have examined the nature of the Bible as inspired, authoritative, inerrant, infallible, necessary, sufficient, and clear, we turn our attention to its function. What does the Bible do? Not surprisingly, what the Bible *does* follows logically from what the Bible *is*.

The Bible is meant to transform us. The Holy Spirit authored the Bible not just so that we could *know things* but so that we could *know God* and be transformed by Him. By the Spirit's work, the Bible grows our relationship with the God it proclaims and transforms us into the image of Christ. We call this the doctrine of illumination, which is closely related to and inseparable from the doctrine of inspiration. The text the

Holy Spirit inspires is also the text the Holy Spirit employs to illuminate our hearts and minds to know and love God. The purpose of the Bible is not merely for communication about God but also for communion with God. We aren't just meant to know about Him, but to know Him.

This is why preachers preach and teachers teach. This is why Christians practice regular reading and meditation on God's Word. This is why we gather together for Bible studies, Sunday school classes, and the Word proclaimed in church. We do all of these things not just to know Scripture better but to better know the one who makes Himself known in Scripture.

The Holy Spirit does not illumine Scripture in the sense that it is darkened and in need of light. The Holy Spirit illumines our darkened hearts and minds so we can understand and be transformed by Scripture. Put another way, the Holy Spirit still speaks what He has spoken. Thus, the Word of God is truly living and active. The Bible is not just a text that informs us but a text that transforms us. When we open our Bibles, the Holy Spirit meets us there. He is not interested in our simply knowing more things but in knowing Him. What does the Bible do? It invites us to know and love God.

In the movie *The Sixth Sense,* we find a plot twist that reveals the living are actually dead. In the Bible we find a plot twist that restores the dead to life. The living and active Word shouts what the creation whispers: there is a God, and you are made to commune with Him. These precious words are, for all who believe, a source of daily bread and a means of daily delight.

You Are a Theologian

Discuss

1. What personal experience have you had with general revelation? Describe the most worshipful moment you have had in nature or the most worshipful non-manmade place you have been.

2. Which of the seven attributes of Scripture is easiest for you to understand and affirm? Which is the hardest? Why?

3. As you read this chapter, what additional passages of Scripture came to mind that support the doctrine of revelation?

4. How has your relationship with the Bible drawn you into deeper relationship with God? What passages are most precious to you? Why?

Pray

Write a prayer thanking God that He has made Himself known, though He was not obligated to do so. Thank Him specifically for a way the Spirit has transformed you through the Scriptures. Confess any hesitation, lack of discipline, or lack of desire you may have toward reading the Bible. Ask Him to help you see His splendor in creation and in His Word this week. Praise Him for the great gift of revelation.

CHAPTER 5

Who Are We?

Anthropology: The Doctrine of Humanity

Brief Definition: *All humans are creatures made in the image of God, either male or female, with the task of representing God to all of His creation.*

Survivor. Real Housewives. The Bachelor. We live in a day where the pervasive appeal of reality TV is a foregone conclusion. But in 1998, as the genre was just beginning to emerge, a prescient movie called *The Truman Show* hit theaters. It portrayed the life of Truman Burbank, a man who, unbeknown to him, lived his entire life from the day he was born on a giant TV set with every aspect of his life carefully scripted. Truman was a human experiment in a hidden camera reality TV show, watched obsessively by millions all around the globe.

The movie masterfully points to our love of voyeurism, even when we know the story we are peering at is, by all reasonable measures, false. Truman at last learns the secret of his existence. Rejecting the false story, he embarks on a perilous journey to the limits of his contrived world and steps out of his soundstage existence into the glaring sunshine of reality. True man at last.

As *The Truman Show* suggests, the audience loves watching "reality" because we are searching for answers to fundamental questions about humanity: What makes people tick? Why do they do the things they do? But more than that, reality shows appeal to our desire to understand those around us so we can come to terms with our own existential questions: What makes *me* tick? Why do *I* do the things I do?

We call the study of humanity "anthropology," from the Greek word *anthropos*, meaning "human." The doctrine of anthropology establishes the intrinsic value and essential purpose of every human being. Before we turn our attention to the question of human significance and purpose, take a minute to remember how the matter of origins played into our understanding of the doctrine of Scripture. The Bible, we noted, was breathed out by God. He is its origin. We understand the Bible's nature and purpose in light of that origin. The Bible is inerrant because God is free from error. The Bible is relational because God is relational. And so on.

The doctrine of anthropology is also indelibly shaped by the matter of origins. Job 33:4 says, "The Spirit of God has made me, and the breath of the Almighty gives me life." Humans are breathed to life by God. He is our origin. We understand our nature and purpose in light of that origin. God forms us as embodied creatures. He makes us in His image. And He gives us work to do. Because He is our Maker, He has the right to determine not just how we are made but for what purpose we are made. Because He is good, His design and His purpose are good.

If you're familiar with the creation account in Genesis 1, you know it says exactly that. On the sixth and final day of creation, humankind is formed in God's image, both male and female, and tasked with ruling and subduing the earth. And God pronounces His crowning work *very good*.

You Are Not Your Own

"Who am I?" is a question humans have asked for as long as there have been humans. No matter the period of human history, no matter the profession or geographical location, ethnicity, or age, everyone wrestles with the question of identity. It's a simple question, with both simple and complex answers. In our current cultural moment, we answer questions of identity in ways that indicate a denial of the matter of origins. We answer subjectively, from person to person, with no sense of having been made by Someone, for one another, for a particular purpose. In our consideration of general revelation, we learned that all humanity has sufficient knowledge of God to acknowledge Him as Creator. Self-determination is fundamentally a denial of our Creator-creature relationship. It believes that identity is achieved, not received.

This is exactly what a serpent promised those first two image-bearers. Don't focus on what you've been given; focus on what has been withheld. Don't do it His way. Do it your way. He's holding back good things from you. *Very good* things.

But as human history would bear out, self-determination is self-delusion. It promises freedom, but it yields bondage. Whether we acknowledge it or not, the most elemental parts of our identity are received, not achieved. Our identity is rooted in how God made us and in what God speaks over us, not in what we make of ourselves. And the implications of this are massive.

God Is the Creator, We Are His Creatures

We have all heard stories of the lucky thrifter who bought a painting at a thrift store for ten dollars, only to discover it was a Rembrandt worth millions. We know from human experience that the value of something is linked to its creator. If we do not consider origin, we will assign value wrongly, and we will assign purpose wrongly. The same is true for human beings. Just as a

Rembrandt does not belong on the back wall of a thrift store at a bargain price, human beings can only understand their identity and purpose when they understand their origin.

The psalmist declares, "Acknowledge that the LORD is God. He made us, and we are his—his people, the sheep of his pasture" (Ps. 100:3). In our discussion of the doctrine of God, we noted that John Calvin argued that the identity of God and our identities are irrevocably intertwined. He claims, "Nearly all the wisdom we possess, that is to say, true and sound wisdom, consists of two parts: the knowledge of God and of ourselves." Calvin's insight frees us from the burden of creating an identity for ourselves by pointing us to an identity found primarily in the one who created us. In order to understand our identity in the deepest possible ways, we have to look to our origin.

Immediately on recognizing that God is our Creator, we gain knowledge of ourselves (and everything else we can perceive) as *created*. Scripture opens with the declaration, "In the beginning God created the heavens and the earth" (Gen. 1:1). Everything that exists—birds, plants, mountains, animals, spiritual beings, and humanity—all things find their origin in God. All created things owe their existence to their Creator. God is the Creator and we are His creation. The first distinction the Bible makes is between the Creator and His creation. When we lose sight of this distinction, we sin as those Paul describes in Romans 1—we worship the creation instead of the One who made it.

As humans, we are called to embrace our humanity and our creatureliness. To be a human is to be a creature. And to be a creature is to be subjected to limits. God is unlimited, and we are limited. We don't like this. When we rail against our natural limits, we are denying our creatureliness. When we believe ourselves to be self-determining and self-ruled, we steal the glory and authority that are due to God.

We Are Image-Bearers

All created things owe their existence to their Creator. But His day 6 creative work is distinctly different from the work of the previous days. On that day, humankind is created unlike birds and beasts and rocks and seas. Humankind is created in the image of God:

> Then God said, "Let us make man in our image, according to our likeness. They will rule the fish of the sea, the birds of the sky, the livestock, the whole earth, and the creatures that crawl on the earth."
>
> So God created [humankind]
> in his own image;
> he created him in the image of God;
> he created them male and female.
> (Gen. 1:26–27)

Though we share something in common with the rest of creation—namely, that we are not God—we are distinguished from the rest of God's creation in a significant respect. Nothing else in all of creation carries the identity or purpose of image-bearer.

Humanity does not just *have* the image of God, as if it is something accidental or something we can lose; humans *are* the image of God. Image-bearing is not something that is tangential to being human but fundamental. It is at the very core of every single human to bear God's image.

But what does it mean to bear God's image? Does it mean we look like Him? How can we look like an invisible God? To bear God's image means that humans reflect what is true about an infinite God in limited human form. Sin's consequences have obscured the image of God in us. We don't reflect Him as we were created to do. But to understand what we were created to "look like," we can look to Christ, the perfect image-bearer. Jesus shows us what it looks like to perfectly reflect the image of God in limited human form.

The concept of image-bearing is not unique to the worldview of the Bible. Other ancient cultures believed that humans could bear the image of a god. They believed specific humans bore the image of the gods and were uniquely chosen to reign and rule on behalf of their gods. However, image-bearing was limited to a certain kind of person—kings and queens. In the ancient world, image-bearing and divine dignity were reserved for royalty alone.

The pharaoh of the Exodus account was thought to be the living image of the sun god Ra and was worshipped as such. In Jesus's day, the emperor Tiberius was worshipped as a god. The customary declaration of "Caesar is Lord" was spoken to reinforce his connection to deity.

Image-bearing was a privileged status in ancient times. And it is in modern times, as well. While contemporary worldviews may not use the terminology of image-bearing, modern-day humans are no less inclined to dignify only certain kinds of humans. We elevate one gender, ethnic group, age demographic, socioeconomic status, or standard of beauty as more worthy of dignity than another.

By contrast, the Bible opposes qualified dignity and instead democratizes it. Rather than reserve the dignity of image-bearing for the *few*, it proclaims it for *all* humans. The Bible utters an unequivocal "no" to any form of qualified dignity. The image of God is not limited in any way to a particular kind of human. All humans are endowed with dignity from their Creator. Hence, the Bible's many warnings against showing favoritism. When we understand that every human bears intrinsic worth because of origin and design, we become better equipped to love our neighbor as we love ourselves.

There is no such thing as conditionality to image-bearing, and that means there is no such thing as conditional dignity.

Image-bearing is not based on usefulness. Image-bearing is not based on ability. Image-bearing is not based on productivity or contribution. Image-bearing means that all humans, regardless of social, intellectual, or physical distinctions, are endowed with divine dignity, value, and worth. Every single person you have ever met bears God's image.

Christians, of all people, hold the opportunity and responsibility to recognize and champion the dignity of all people. In a world that seeks to dehumanize, Christians are called to rehumanize all people. We rehumanize our neighbors. We rehumanize the oppressed. We rehumanize our political enemies. We rehumanize the unbeliever and the antagonist of our faith. The Bible invites Christians to see humanity as "us" and not as "other." And so does the example of Christ.

Our Bodies Matter

God could have made us to bear His image in any way He chose. His sovereign choice was that we should do so in a physical body. We are created both physical and spiritual, possessing both bodies and souls. In this way we are distinct from other living creatures—from plants, from birds, and yes, (deep breaths) even from our much-loved pets. Humanity is the place where the material and the spiritual are joined together.

Not every worldview holds to a dual emphasis on the spiritual and material. Some emphasize the spiritual nature of humanity to the neglect of the physical. In the history of theological discourse, this view is known as *gnosticism*. Gnosticism holds that humans are not their bodies but simply their souls. A person is a soul currently housed in a body. The body is an unfortunate add-on that will hopefully be discarded one day.

Other worldviews emphasize the physical nature of humanity to the neglect of the immaterial. This view is called *materialism*. According to materialists, humans do not have souls, or immaterial parts, but can be entirely explained by physical matter. An overemphasis on the physical nature of humans leads to the view that we are nothing more than our bodies. Once our bodies decline and die, we no longer exist.

By contrast, the Bible teaches that we are our bodies and we are our souls. As image-bearers, all humans are both body and soul, each part being essential to what it is to be a human.

Bodies and Souls, Male and Female

One key area where this body and soul dichotomy informs Christian theology is in relationship to gender and sexuality. The joining of who we are on the inside to who we are on the outside is the work of our good Creator. And our good Creator has ordained that His image would be displayed through both male and female. The Bible maintains the importance of both our shared humanity and our differentiated sex.

First, consider the distinction that both men and women bear God's image. As we saw in Genesis 1:27 (ESV), "God created man [humanity] in his own image, in the image of God he created him; male and female he created them." Both male and female share equally in the status of divine image-bearing. In the next chapter of Genesis, we gain even more insight into their shared status as image-bearers.

We have touched on the story of Adam naming the animals as an example of ordering and taxonomizing. Now let's revisit that story to see what it tells us about men and women both made in God's image:

> Now out of the ground the LORD God had formed every beast of the field and every bird of the heavens and brought them to the man to see what he would call them. And whatever the man called every living creature, that was its name. The man gave names to all livestock and to the birds of the heavens and to every beast of the field. But for Adam there was not found a helper fit for him. (Gen. 2:19–20 ESV)

Note the learning drawn from Adam's naming of the animals: there is no other creature *like him*. Though every animal he names has others according to its kind, he does not. The other creatures have corresponding partners, but there is no corresponding partner for Adam. There is not a helper fit for him. His taxonomizing work yields the stark realization that he is profoundly alone. He has no partner for the mission that God has given him.

Adam realizes there is a difference, not in degree but in kind between himself and every other creature. He is missing a co-image-bearer, a necessary ally. But God stands ready with a remedy:

> Then the LORD God said, "It is not good that the man should be alone; I will make him a helper fit for him." . . . So the LORD God caused a deep sleep to fall upon the man, and while he slept took one of his ribs and closed up its place with flesh. And the rib that the LORD God had taken from the man he made into a woman and brought her to the man. Then the man said,
>
> > "This at last is bone of my bones
> > and flesh of my flesh;
> > she shall be called Woman,
> > because she was taken out of Man."
>
> (Gen. 2:18, 21–23 ESV)

Notice Adam's first response when he meets Eve. He does not exclaim how different she is from him in her sexuality, though there are important differences. His first instinct is that she is *like him*. At last! Bone of my bones. At last! Flesh of my flesh. Adam receives the gift of Eve, someone who is like him. They share a significant and fundamental sameness: they both bear the image of God.

But it is not just their sameness that remedies the "not good" pronouncement of Genesis 2:18. It is also their distinction from each other. Genesis 1:27 articulates both sameness and differentiation: humanity is made in God's image, but humanity is also distinguishable as male and female. Though men and women share more in common than what separates them—equality in personhood, shared mission, and divine image-bearing—they are not interchangeable. Male is male, and female is female.

This differentiation is what will enable them to partner in their purpose. The first humans are told to "be fruitful and multiply and fill the earth and subdue it" (Gen. 1:28). Without male and female, the mission of multiplication cannot be accomplished.

As it was in the garden, so it is today. Each individual, male or female, is created in the image of God. Each individual is given a body differentiated by sex. Humanity cannot bear God's image to the next generation apart from the contributions of both sexes. When we distort, overlook, or erase human sexuality as God created it, we participate in attempting to overturn God's created order.

As Paul notes in Romans 9, we are pots formed by the Potter. Rather than ask, "Why have you made me thus?," we submit to His infinitely superior wisdom and insight, trusting His good purposes in giving us the physical body we have been given.

Made to Represent, Made to Rule

God creates us in His image, male and female. He gives us an identity. But He also gives us a purpose. A mission. A task. But what is it?

The Bible tells us that the purpose of humanity is to represent God to all of creation. Immediately after "let us make humans in our image," we hear this purpose articulated:

> "They will rule the fish of the sea, the birds
> of the sky, the livestock, the whole earth,
> and the creatures that crawl on the earth."
> (Gen. 1:26)

First the mission is spoken over them; then it is spoken to them:

God blessed them, and God said to them,
"Be fruitful, multiply, fill the earth, and subdue it. Rule the fish of the sea, the birds of
the sky, and every creature that crawls on the
earth." (Gen. 1:28)

The purpose of humanity is to extend the glory of God
to all of creation. Just as their body/soul dichotomy sets them
apart from the rest of creation, so does their vocation. God's
command to the first humans is known as the "cultural mandate." A *mandate* is simply a command. The word *cultural* is
used in the same sense as a cultured pearl versus a freshwater
pearl. Cultured pearls have been intentionally shaped to be
round versus asymmetrical. Thus, the term *cultural mandate*
means "a command to order what is disordered."

When God gives the cultural mandate to humankind, He
invites them to join Him in the work He has begun in the
six days of creation: the ordering of chaos. The God who has
ordered light and darkness, sea and dry land, plants and animals now tasks those who reflect Him in their embodiment
to reflect Him in their vocation.

It is the unique job or vocation that is given to no other
part of God's creation but humanity. In the cultural mandate, humanity is commissioned by God Himself to rule over
His creation—the land, the sea, the air—and to represent His
glory to all. Humans bear the image of God in their work

by ordering what is disordered. This means even the most mundane tasks can be infused with supernatural meaning: doing yard work, creating a filing system, changing a diaper, cleaning a kitchen floor, making a shopping list. Every act of ordering is an act of ruling.

The Bible presents God as King over all His creation. But it also presents humanity as vice-regents, or mini-kings and queens, through whom God extends His authority to His creation. To be an image-bearer is to be royalty, but royalty with a purpose. Humanity's task is to represent God by extending His sovereign and gracious rule to all He has made. Our representation of Him is for His glory, not for our own. Every act of ruling by an image-bearer is meant to reflect God, not to rival Him. We were not created to be Babel-builders, seeking our own glory. In all our labor, we labor as unto the Lord.

This is exactly what Christ did. Any conversation about image-bearing that does not end with Jesus Christ is insufficient. "He is the image of the invisible God, the firstborn over all creation" (Col. 1:15). He is "the radiance of God's glory and the exact expression of his nature" (Heb. 1:3 ESV). It is into the image of Christ that Christ-followers are being conformed (Rom. 8:29). Jesus is the true image-bearer, who perfectly rules on God's behalf and represents Him perfectly. Though the image was obscured in us by sin, it is becoming clearer and clearer again as we are made to look more and more like Jesus. As we grow in our sanctification, we see the image of God reemerge from obscurity. And we become increasingly truly human, as we were created to be.

Like Truman Burbank, we were all born into a world where the truth is out there, though it has been obscured from our sight by a constructed reality. Unlike Truman, we are told to become willing prisoners of our own constructed reality. We are told to live our own individual truth, to be self-defined. The Bible beckons us to press beyond all the available false narratives of who we are and why we are here. But the act of rediscovery may be both painful and costly. A biblically informed doctrine of humankind is contested in our society perhaps more than any other doctrine we will study. Hostility awaits anyone who openly violates the civil orthodoxy regarding gender, race, and any other issue of identity.

"Into an age screaming for me to live my truth, the Scriptures speak calmly that my truth, self-declared and self-defined, is a lie."[8] But my Maker's truth transcends. My Creator's truth endures. It is an anchor in a storm-tossed world, beaten to and fro on the waves of faddish culture. The doctrine of anthropology reminds us that we are not our own. Another has crafted our frame. Another has charted our course. He is trustworthy and true. And in the light of His truth, we at last become the humans we were created to be.

You Are a Theologian

Discuss

1. We are creatures, and creatures have limits. What are some ways you are currently experiencing your limitations? In what areas of your life is God inviting you to embrace your limits?

2. Human history demonstrates that we are prone to fail to see the dignity of every image-bearer. Why do you think this is so?

3. Who are you most tempted to devalue? Why? Who is easiest for you to value? Why?

4. In your own experience of the body/soul dichotomy, which aspect have you tended to emphasize more?

5. What aspect of your daily work have you not perceived as an opportunity for you to reflect the glory of God because of its mundane nature? What aspect of your daily work are you most prone to seek glory from?

Pray

Write a prayer praising God for His creative work in making humans to bear His image. Confess to Him when your view of your own value or the value of others has fallen short of what it should. Praise Him that your everyday labors are not an obligation but an effort of eternal significance. Ask Him to expose favoritism in your heart, to give you joy in your work and relationships, and to fix your eyes on Christ. Thank Him for sending Jesus to show us what image-bearing means and to open a way for us to be restored.

CHAPTER 6

What Went Wrong?

Hamartiology: The Doctrine of Sin

Brief Definition: *Humanity, created in God's image to represent Him, sins and rebels against Him resulting in exile, depravity, and death.*

"Houston, we have a problem." No doubt, these were not the words astronaut Jim Lovell most wanted to be remembered by. On the heels of two prior successful lunar landings, he and the crew of *Apollo 13* hoped eagerly for their own successful mission, but when an oxygen tank failed, the plan had to be scrapped.

Lovell's terse comment to mission control became famous because it was so understated in comparison to the actual problem. The crew did not yet grasp the full consequences of the catastrophic failure of the tank, but they would spend the next several days fighting for their lives, learning its consequences, and trying to get back home.

Just three chapters in, the Bible introduces a story of catastrophic failure. A serpent appears in a well-ordered garden with an alternate plan to the one God has set in place. The first two humans exchange the truth of God for a lie. Though created as God's royal image-bearers and commissioned to reign and rule as His representatives, they trade submission for self-rule. Instead of making God's name great, they choose to make a name for themselves. Instead of the work of building God's kingdom, they choose to build on their own terms. In response, God articulates the tragic consequences of their sin and rebellion. Of our sin and rebellion: exile, depravity, and death.

Humanity, we have a problem. The rest of the Bible, and indeed, the rest of human history, will be a story of reckoning with the fallout of the sin catastrophe, looking for a way to get home.

Genesis 3 asks and answers questions all humans must grapple with: Why is the world filled with suffering and injustice? What went wrong? And just how bad is the problem?

In Christian theology, these questions are addressed in the doctrine of sin. We call the study of the doctrine of sin "hamartiology," from the Greek word *hamartia*, meaning "sin." The doctrine of sin examines our rebellion against God and its consequences of exile, depravity, and death.

What Went Wrong?

Rebellion

You may be familiar with the words of Romans 3:23: "All have sinned and fall short of the glory of God." The events of Genesis 3 chronicle that fall. And they give us a working definition of sin. We tend to think of sin as just "doing something wrong." But Genesis 3 shows us that sin is rebellion, and sin is relational.

Adam and Eve were not ignorant of God's commands. In Genesis 2, God commands His image-bearers: "You are free to eat from any tree of the garden, but you must not eat from the tree of the knowledge of good and evil, for on the day you eat from it, you will certainly die" (Gen. 2:16–17). This command from God was meant for our good, but only one chapter later humanity begins to seek good outside of the command of the Lord.

In Genesis 3 we learn that a cunning serpent enters the garden of Eden in order to deceive humanity. The serpent convinces them that what God said was not actually for their good. That God was holding out on them. The serpent convinces humanity to eat of the tree God commanded them not to eat from. The serpent contradicts the Word of the Lord, and the humans listen to the word of the serpent.

Sin is rebelling against God and His created order. Sin is believing God is foolish and we are wise. Listening to the Word of the Lord conforms us to the image of God. Listening to the word of the liar conforms us to the image of the serpent. Sin is disordered affections and distorted knowledge. We do not love what is lovely, and we do not know what is good. And we do not look like or live like those made in the image of God.

The Bible recounts our traitorous decision: "The woman saw that the tree was good for food and delightful to look at, and that it was desirable for obtaining wisdom. So she took some of its fruit and ate it; she also gave some to her husband, who was with her, and he ate it" (Gen. 3:6).

Sin is rebellion because it elevates our will above God's. It is looking for a better title and a better task, tragically failing to realize that God has already given us the greatest title and task we could have. Instead of embracing our rightful title and task, we wanted something more. We chose rivalry rather than representation, placing ourselves on the throne rather than revering and representing its rightful occupant.

Exile

Sin is relational because it impacts our relationship with God, with self, and with one another, and even with creation as a whole. It separates us from our Maker, obscures our identity, and frustrates our shared purpose of fulfilling the cultural mandate. In the wake of their disastrous decision, God confronts them and illuminates for them the consequences of their rebellion: pain in childbearing, sweat and thorns in the work of cultivation, competition instead of collaboration, a return to the dust from which they had been formed. And exile from His presence:

> The LORD God said, "Since the man has become like one of us, knowing good and evil, he must not reach out, take from the tree of life, eat, and live forever." So the LORD God sent him away from the garden of Eden to work the ground from which he was taken. He drove the man out and stationed the cherubim and the flaming, whirling sword east of the garden of Eden to guard the way to the tree of life. (Gen. 3:22–24)

God uses their exile to remind them there is a home they long for. Humans who were made to enjoy the presence of God are cast out from the presence of God.

Sent out. Driven out. That is where we are. The consequences of our sin are life without God. Working the ground without Him, looking for life outside of Him. In the final devastating lines of Genesis 3, humanity is expelled from God's presence.

Exile is not just a one-time event but a pattern that continues throughout the story of Scripture. Israel's story is marked by wilderness, exile, and Babylon—life in a Genesis 3 world is life east of Eden. We are all exiles looking for and longing for the presence of God. Even the New Testament church is a group of elect exiles (1 Pet. 1:1). We were made to enjoy the presence of God, and our only hope is that God would come and end our exile and bless us with His presence again.

How Bad Is It?

We cannot fully grasp the impact of sin without the framework of how things were before sin entered the picture. Only with a clear vision of the beauty and order of Genesis 1 and 2 can we rightly understand the horror and devastation of Genesis 3. The memory of Eden's perfection is what fuels our longing for all things to be made new.

Think for a moment about the tragic stories you know of or have experienced firsthand. Now think of the ones you have heard about in your church. In your community. In your country. In the world in the past two weeks. In the world in the past one hundred years, five hundred years, two thousand years. Every single tragedy finds its birth narrative in Genesis 3. Every human failure, every broken promise, every errant word, every deceitful act, every abuse, every heinous crime, every act of neglect, every miscarriage of justice, every dark behavior can be traced back to the fall in Genesis 3. Disease, sickness, poverty, mental illness, famine, war. After two chapters in paradise—image-bearing, dignity, worth, purpose—we are confronted with a universal and catastrophic tragedy.

It is hard to imagine a more tragic fall. We were meant to bring order to chaos but instead brought chaos into God's order.

The sin of our parents Adam and Eve affected humans, but it also affected every part of creation. God tells Adam, "Cursed is the ground because of you" (Gen. 3:17 ESV). Paul speaks of the pervasive nature of this curse:

> For the creation was subjected to futility—
> not willingly, but because of him who sub-
> jected it—in the hope that the creation
> itself will also be set free from the bondage
> to decay into the glorious freedom of God's
> children. For we know that the whole cre-
> ation has been groaning together with labor
> pains until now. (Rom. 8:20–22)

As we look around at decay and desolation in the created order, we can know that indeed we need new heavens and a new earth.

Obstacles and encumbrances now bar our good work. Sorrow and suffering now cloud our contentment. Envy and enmity now corrupt our communion with one another. Decay and desolation now corrode our landscape.

In Adam, All Die

But why is the sin of Adam and Eve our problem? Why don't the consequences of their sin stop with them? The Bible describes Adam and Eve's sin not only as *theirs* but also as *ours*. The original sin does not belong just to Adam and Eve but to all of us. How can this be? Paul emphasizes this in his letter to the Romans: "Therefore, just as sin entered the world through one man, and death through sin, in this way death spread to all people, because all sinned" (Rom. 5:12). Death entered the world through disobedience, our disobedience in Adam. We were there. We were complicit. We participated.

We don't like the idea of Adam as our representative. We tell ourselves we ought not to be held responsible for his mistake. But if God is indeed sovereign and good, then His choice of Adam for this role is the best choice. He was a justly chosen representative, despite the outcome. We can know that, had we been in that garden, the outcome would have been the same. Otherwise, we have indeed been dealt with unjustly in the matter of representation.

Depravity

The doctrine of total depravity teaches that our nature, human nature, underwent a fundamental transformation in the fall of Adam and Eve. Sin is a contagion, and we have all been infected. The term *total depravity* does not mean that we are totally depraved in our thoughts or behaviors but that sin infects every aspect of our being. Because of Adam's sin, all humans are born predisposed to sin. We are not born morally neutral. We are still born as image-bearers, but we are born "in Adam" (1 Cor. 15:22), with a distorted nature that leads inexorably to sinful behavior. To put it a bit differently, we sin not just because of nurture but of nature.

We are born in Adam, but new life comes from being born again in the second Adam—Christ. "For just as in Adam all die, so also in Christ all will be made alive" (1 Cor 15:22). The fall destroys our ability to not sin. The cross restores it.

The fourth-century theologian Augustine offers helpful categories for how we relate to sin through different ages in redemptive history:

Pre-Fall Humanity	Post-Fall Humanity	Post-Conversion	Post-Return of Christ
Able to not sin	Not able to not sin	Able to not sin	Not able to sin

- **Before the fall:** In the garden of Eden, God created all things good. That includes our nature. Adam and Eve had a nature that was able to obey God and not sin.

- **After the fall:** After the fall, Adam and Eve, and all of their family (including us) are born with a sinful nature. This does not mean that all we do is sin all the time. Instead, it means that we are unable to walk in perfect obedience due to our depraved state.

- **Post-conversion:** Part of the good news of the gospel is that after the death, burial, and resurrection of Christ He sends us His Spirit. Not only is our sin forgiven, but our natures are being restored. Not only does the Spirit grant us eternal life, but He also empowers us to live holy lives. We still do not obey perfectly, but the presence of the Spirit means we have been empowered, through the gospel, to live lives of obedience.

- **In the kingdom:** A day is coming when Jesus will make all things new. We will no longer live in a broken world, and our sinful nature will be completely restored. Sin and death will be no more.

Death

The consequences of our rebellion are not just exile and depravity, but also very real spiritual and physical death. God commands Adam not to eat from the tree in the garden lest he surely die (Gen. 2:17). Gazing at each other immediately after eating the fruit, still breathing in and out, Adam and Eve might have believed the serpent to be the truth-teller. But God's word does not fail. The genealogies of Genesis name a man's name, number his years, and sound the repeating knell: "and then he died." Over and over again. God is not a man that He should lie (Num. 23:19).

In creation, God takes humanity up out of the dust, forming us, and breathing life into us. In the fall, humanity is returned to whence he came. From dust to dust. Death is a reversal of God's good created order. "The wages of sin is death" (Rom. 6:23).

Death is the great enemy that, since the garden's catastrophic event, has plagued all of humanity. The prophet Isaiah speaks of death being "the covering that is cast over all peoples, the view that is spread over all nations," and that one day, God, "will swallow up death forever; and the Lord GOD will wipe away tears from all faces, and the reproach of his people he will take away from all the earth" (Isa. 25:7–8 ESV). Paul reminds us that death is the final enemy of God to be abolished (1 Cor. 15:26).

But why does this matter to you personally? It matters because we can all agree there is something wrong— something wrong in the world and something wrong in us. But if we don't know what the problem is, we won't know what the solution is. Understanding what the problem is means everything. Like a doctor examining a patient with a disease. If a doctor misdiagnoses the disease, they will inevitably mistreat it.

It is one thing to have an understanding of the concept of sinfulness; it is another to personalize it. To think specifically of how each of us has rebelled against God's holiness. How we have lied, stolen, cheated, hated, and lusted, and how we, just like our first parents, are often found hiding behind the trees, hoping nobody will see our depravity.

Sin is not just a theological concept. It is personal. It has impacted each and every one of us. Sin is something each of us knows far too much about. We have been sinned against, and we have sinned against God and others. The world would have us believe that the greatest problems in the world are external to us, but the Bible tells us the greatest problem is in all of us.

There is a famous story that in the 1900s the *London Times* posed a question to several prominent scholars and authors, "What is wrong with the world?" Various types of responses were offered: health care, education, human rights. G. K. Chesterton offered this response: "Dear Sir, I am."

If we externalize all that is wrong with the world, we will believe the solution is inside of us. Try harder. Work smarter. Be better. Do the work. Pick yourself up by the bootstraps. But when we realize the problem is in us—all of us—we realize the solution must be outside of us. We need someone to come and save us. When we personalize sin, we realize we no longer need to hide behind the trees but to embrace the Man who hung on the cursed tree in our place.

Humans are people of the dust, made in God's image for the purpose of representing Him to all of His creation. Our refusal to submit ourselves to His good rule has led to exile, depravity, and death.

The saga of the *Apollo 13* lunar launch ends not in disaster but in deliverance. Their story of calling, catastrophe, striving, and safe passage resolved in a matter of days. And though we know not the day or the hour, so will ours, for those of us in Christ. Our only hope is that one day, God will make all things right. That our exile will end so we can enjoy the presence of God forever. That our depravity will be healed so we can live in obedience to God. And that, one day death will be defeated, so we can stand over the grave of death, mocking it, declaring: "Death is swallowed up in victory." "O death, where is your victory? O death, where is your sting?" (1 Cor. 15:54–55 ESV).

You Are a Theologian

Discuss

1. How have you seen the catastrophic effects of sin in your own life or in the life of someone you love? What current circumstance makes you long the most for the end of sin and death?

2. How comfortable are you with the idea of original sin, that Adam represented you and all humanity in the fall? What thoughts contribute to your discomfort? To your acceptance?

3. Before we sin, Satan assures us our sin has no consequence; after we sin, he convinces us our sin is unforgivable. How have you found this to be true in your own life?

4. How might the habit of confession of sin be an act of bringing order out of the chaos of sin's effects? How should confession shape our attitude toward our sin and the sin of others?

5. How might the habit of forgiving those who sin against us be an act of bringing order out of the chaos of sin's effects? How should forgiveness shape our attitude toward our sin and the sin of others?

Pray

Meditate on the Lord's Prayer phrase by phrase. After each phrase, note how your understanding of the doctrine of sin shapes the beauty and usefulness of this model prayer. Then pray the Lord's Prayer aloud to Him, adding your reflections.

> Our Father in heaven,
> your name be honored as holy.
> Your kingdom come.
> Your will be done
> on earth as it is in heaven.
> Give us today our daily bread.
> And forgive us our debts,
> as we also have forgiven our debtors.
> And do not bring us into temptation,
> but deliver us from the evil one.
> (Matt. 6:9–13)

CHAPTER 7

What Has God Done? (Part 1)

The Doctrines of Christology, Atonement, and Justification

Brief Definition: *The eternal Son of God was sent by the Father, taking on a human nature, in order to accomplish salvation for sinful humanity in His life, death, burial, resurrection, and ascension.*

Have you ever found yourself in need of rescue? Have you ever been in a situation where your life was in the hands of another?

In the summer of 2018, a youth football team in Thailand finished their practice and followed their coach into a nearby cave for swimming and recreational time together. Little did they know, as they traversed through the cave, a monsoon was trapping them further and further in, with no way out. Ranging in age from eleven to twenty-five, with no diving gear, they were completely blocked off from the rest of the world. Death loomed with certainty.

After more than a week of rescue efforts, a team of divers was able to locate the trapped team. They were alive but miles away from the opening of the cave. Huddled together on a rock, they awaited their fate. In a race with time, thousands of people joined in the rescue attempt. Professional divers, government agencies, soldiers, helicopters, and ambulances were all deployed in the effort.

Nine days to locate the team, eight days to bring them out one by one. Through muddy waters, tight passageways, and darkness, professional divers led each member of the team to safety. Against the odds, the seventeen-day ordeal ended in a successful rescue of the boys and their coach. But not without cost. Two members of the rescue team lost their lives. The world of search and rescue is marked by self-sacrifice.

The doctrine of sin teaches us that our rebellion has led to sin, exile, depravity, and death—we need rescue. In a sense, we are trapped. Our lives are on the line. We are in desperate need of someone coming to our rescue. Now, with the doctrine of Christology, we turn our eyes to what that rescue requires and how it is accomplished. More precisely, we turn

WHAT HAS GOD DONE? (PART 1)

our eyes to a Person, able to save, willing to lay down His life for ours, to bring us from the kingdom of darkness to the kingdom of light.

Incarnation: He Took on Flesh

When we speak of the good news of our salvation, the gospel, we speak often of the cross of Christ. But the significance of the crucifixion emerges as it is set in its context. Before we can understand the significance of that death, we must first meditate on the significance of the life that preceded it. Before we can speak of the forgiveness of sin, we must speak of the person who made forgiveness of sin possible. Before we can treasure the cross, we must treasure the incarnation.

If you grew up with the Christmas tradition of setting up a manger scene, you have participated in a simple act of treasuring the incarnation. We may debate the historical accuracy of whether there was a donkey in the next stall or when the wise men arrived, but Christians all agree on the baby in that scene. Jesus, the God-Man is there. Pink toes, swaddling cloths, living, and breathing. That is what we are celebrating at Christmas. The King has come to save us, God in the flesh.

You'll recall our definition of God the Trinity from a previous chapter: *God eternally exists as one essence and three distinct persons, God the Father, God the Son, and God the Holy Spirit. Each person is fully God, yet there is one God.* In this chapter, we are looking specifically at the implications of God the Father sending God the Son to become *incarnate* in order to accomplish *salvation* on our behalf.

The gospel is not just what Jesus came to do but who Jesus is. Christianity centers around not only what Jesus accomplished (our salvation), but on the one who accomplished it (the Son of God incarnate). The word *incarnate* means "embodied in flesh." But the Christian concept of incarnation includes not just the taking on of a body but of a human nature. In other words, Jesus possessed a human body, soul, mind, and will.

In the incarnation, the eternal Son of God is sent by the Father to take to Himself a human nature, in order to accomplish salvation on our behalf. The Son of God assumes, or adds to Himself, a human nature. This act makes Jesus Christ the God-Man. Two natures, one divine and one human, in one person.

John's Gospel opens by announcing the divinity of Jesus:

> In the beginning was the Word, and the Word was with God, and the Word *was* God. He was with God in the beginning. All things were created through him, and apart from him not one thing was created that has been created. In him was life, and that life was the light of men. (John 1:1–4, emphasis added)

Don't miss what John is saying here. Everything was made through Jesus. He has life in Himself. He is God.

But just a few sentences later, still in the first chapter, John also reminds us of this glorious truth: "The Word became flesh and dwelt among us. We observed his glory, the glory as the one and only Son from the Father, full of grace and truth" (John 1:14).

Basic Christology, or the doctrine of Christ, is:

> Jesus is fully God.
>
> Jesus is fully human, yet without sin.
>
> Jesus is one person.

Theologians call this the *hypostatic union* (or dual nature of Christ), meaning two natures in one person. When we stray from or distort the doctrine of Christ, one of these truths has been compromised.

Consider a handful of heresies the church has addressed in the last two millennia. Jesus did not, when He assumed human nature, empty Himself of divinity (that's a heresy called *kenoticism*, mid-nineteenth century). Jesus did not just seem or appear to be human but was spirit only (*gnosticism*, first to third century). Jesus is not less than divine (*Arianism*, fourth century). Jesus did not only take up physical elements of humanity (*Apollinarianism*, fourth century). Jesus is not two persons (*Nestorianism*, fifth century).

These common misconceptions still populate the pews today to varying degrees, as every generation of believers tries to resolve the tension of the dual nature of Christ. Heresy always seeks to resolve the tension that orthodoxy maintains. Jesus is fully God, fully man, in one person.

This holds significant impact for our understanding of the gospel because our salvation is accomplished by the only person who has ever lived who is fully God and fully man. Because of the incarnation, Jesus becomes the supreme and perfect revelation of God. God is *exactly* like Jesus. Paul tells us that Jesus is the image of the invisible God (Col. 1:15). The author of Hebrews announces that Jesus is the exact imprint of God's nature (Heb. 1:1–4).

That means that if you have a view of God that is inconsistent with Jesus, then you do not have a God that should be worshipped but an idol to be destroyed. God is just like Jesus. What a comfort! When we come to know Jesus, we can be confident that we have come to know God. If we want to know what God is like, we need look no further than Jesus.

Jesus became incarnate to reveal God, but even better, Jesus is God coming to rescue us. The Son was sent not merely for our illumination but for our salvation. And to accomplish that, He had to assume a human nature—a nature in which He became *exactly* like you and me, with one exception: He did not sin.

The Accomplishments of Salvation

Now that we know that Jesus is fully God and fully man, what did Jesus come to accomplish? What did He come to do? If we were to formulate a to-do list for Jesus in the incarnation, it would be this:

- Live a perfectly obedient life.
- Die a substitutionary death for the unrighteous, carrying our sin and shame.
- Be buried in a tomb.
- Rise victoriously, leaving our sin and shame in the tomb.
- Ascend to heaven, to reign as King.

All of these Christ accomplished. Each of these impacts our fundamental understanding of the gospel and deserves closer consideration.

A Life of Perfect Obedience

The time between Christmas and Good Friday in the Bible matters just as much to our doctrine as the inflection points. After Jesus's birth, He grows to an adult and performs His earthly ministry, a period of about thirty-three years. During that span, He lives a perfectly obedient life according to God's law. He breaks not one command. He commits no sin

YOU ARE A THEOLOGIAN

of omission and no sin of commission. He asks forgiveness in the Lord's Prayer to set an example for us, but He has nothing for which to ask forgiveness. "He did not commit sin, and no deceit was found in his mouth" (1 Pet. 2:22). He is fully human yet without sin. He is the only person to accomplish this.

The obedience of Jesus stands in stark contrast to every other human who has ever lived. After the fall, all of humanity is represented by the disobedient one—Adam—and we ourselves walk in the same disobedience. We fail to go weeks, days, hours, or sometimes even minutes without disobeying God's good commands. But every minute of every hour of every day of every month of every year of His life, Jesus was perfectly obedient. Jesus's life was pleasing to the Father (John 8:29). He delighted in God's will (Luke 2:49), had no sin (1 John 3:5), and came to fulfill the law (Matt. 5:17).

His perfect obedience qualifies Him to die in place of the disobedient. It makes Him the spotless lamb, the perfect sacrifice. But it does more than qualify Him to die in our place; it qualifies Him to be the perfect example for us. We fix our eyes on Him; we strive to conform to His image that we may walk as He walked. Not only do we partake in Jesus's death, but we also partake in His life.

Death

In spite of His perfect obedience to God's law, Jesus suffered the curse of the cross, the death of a criminal pronounced guilty. Death is the consequence of sin (Gen. 3:19). Someone who hasn't sinned does not deserve to die. So, why did the obedient One die?

Jesus, the obedient One, died so the disobedient ones may live. Jesus died in our place. "[God] made the one who did not know sin to be sin for us, so that in him we might become the righteousness of God" (2 Cor. 5:21). No wonder we call it "Good Friday."

The doctrine of atonement helps us understand what Jesus's death accomplished. *Atonement* is another word for reconciliation or recompense. It is the means by which we are made right with God. The doctrine of the atonement teaches that Jesus's death accomplished the following:

- It was a substitute for a just penalty.
- It satisfied the wrath of God.
- It cleansed our impurity.
- It granted us righteousness.
- It reconciled us to God forever.
- It defeated death on a cosmic level.

The death of Jesus is a *substitute for a just penalty*. "The wages of sin is death" (Rom. 6:23). God is holy and just, and in order to maintain His justice, the penalty for sin must be paid in full. But because our sins against God require an infinite punishment, no finite being can pay it in full. Without a substitute, sinful humanity spends eternity suffering the consequences of our sin. Only God can substitute Himself in our place to offer a satisfactory sacrifice. So, the perfect Son of God became a human, lived a perfect life, and died in our place as a substitute. This is called *penal substitution*.

At the heart of substitutionary atonement is one word: *for*. Jesus died *for* us. Peter highlights the importance of this word when he says, "Christ also suffered once *for* sins, the righteous *for* the unrighteous, that he might bring us to God" (1 Pet. 3:18 ESV, emphasis added). Do not miss that. Jesus suffered on the cross *for* sins. The righteous *for* the unrighteous. The sinless *for* the sinful. The obedient *for* the disobedient. The guiltless *for* the guilty.

The death of Jesus *satisfies the wrath of God*. God's wrath is justly placed on sinners, those who have rebelled against Him. At the death of Christ, God's wrath is not forgotten or erased; it is exhausted. Through the work of Christ on the cross, the wrath of God is fully satisfied. Paul asserts that Jesus's death is a *propitiatory* death (Rom. 3:23–26). Propitiation is the satisfaction of wrath through the offering of a gift—in this case a blood sacrifice. The imagery Paul invokes is the mercy seat of the ark, the place where priests made atonement for God's people by sacrificing a lamb. The cross is the collision of the justice and mercy of God, saving sinners who could never save themselves. Take this to heart: if you are in Christ, the wrath of God has been completely satisfied, completely exhausted, in His death *for* you.

The death of Jesus *cleanses our impurity*. Your sin has made you unclean, but the blood of Christ washes all of your sin away. Not only is the wrath of God fully appeased, but sinners who were once stained with unrighteousness and impurity are fully cleansed and made pure through the blood of Christ (Heb. 9:13–14; 1 John 1:7, 9).

The death of Jesus *grants us righteousness*. When you think of righteousness, think in judicial terms. The guilty are not just forgiven, though that is true; they are declared innocent. Not only are our sins forgiven, but we are credited the righteousness of Jesus Christ. His righteousness is credited to our account as if it were completely ours (Rom. 4:22–25).

The death of Jesus *reconciles us to God forever*. When you think of reconciliation, think in relational terms. Reconciliation means that, though we were enemies of God, through Christ we have been brought near. Sin says we are born at enmity with God, but salvation says we have been reconciled to God. Colossians 1:22 says, "Now he has reconciled you by his physical body through his death, to present you holy, faultless, and blameless before him." Once God's enemies, the cross declares us friends. Once hostile to God, the cross declares us holy.

The death of Jesus *defeats death on a cosmic level*. Although the death of Jesus is deeply personal, it is also cosmic. He did not just die for you, but in His death He accomplished a victory over cosmic powers of darkness. The death of Christ signals the defeat of every power of darkness in the world, which will be fully realized when Jesus establishes His kingdom on earth, making every enemy His footstool (Ps. 110:1; 1 Cor. 1:25; Heb. 10:13).

Burial

After Jesus's crucifixion, He was laid in a tomb. Just as we can forget the significance of the interval between Advent and Good Friday—Jesus's perfect life, we can forget the significance of the interval between Good Friday and Easter—Jesus's death.

Think of the scene in the movie *The Princess Bride*, where the hero Westley lies stretched on a rack, by all appearances, dead. On close examination, Miracle Max declares him to be "mostly dead." Max observes, "There's a big difference between mostly dead and all dead. Mostly dead is slightly alive." Westley is resuscitated, and the movie continues on its merry way.

That is not how it was with Jesus. He was dead. Fully dead. All dead. His lifeless body had no air pumping through His lungs. No brain function. Completely dead. Because of His full death, we can know we are now fully dead to sin. No chance of resuscitation. Thanks be to God.

Resurrection

After three days, death meets its death. Jesus's body was not resuscitated; it was resurrected. The one who was dead is now alive. At last, Easter.

The cross is not where salvation is accomplished in full. The death of Christ accomplishes nothing if Jesus had remained dead. Not only was He slain for our trespasses, but He was also raised for our justification (Rom. 4:25). He didn't stay in the grave but rose victoriously over sin, Satan, and death.

If Jesus was still in the tomb, we would still be in our sin. Instead, He leaves our sin and guilt dead in the tomb and walks out alive. The resurrection vindicates Jesus and all who belong to Him. It also signifies our future hope: the resurrection was just the firstfruits of all who belong to Him (1 Cor. 15:20). Think about this: the only thing unique about Jesus's resurrection is that He got to go first. All who belong to Jesus will one day emerge victorious from their graves taunting Satan, sin, and death. Death does not have the final word for Christians—resurrection does.

Ascension

Good Friday is not the sum total of salvation. Easter is not the end of the story. Our resurrected Lord, the one who "humbled himself by becoming obedient to the point of death—even to death on a cross" must move from His humiliation to His exaltation (Phil. 2:8). After His resurrection, Jesus presented Himself alive and taught about the kingdom of God for forty days (Acts 1:1–3). But that was not all. The events that transpired after His resurrection showed Him to be not just a teacher about the kingdom, but its ruling King. Right before their eyes, He was lifted up to heaven (Acts 1:9) where He reigns even now and ever more.

Jesus's ascension is a demonstration of His kingship over every single thing. He is not in heaven resting; He is in heaven reigning. He is seated on a throne. He's at the right hand of His Father, highly exalted, having received the name above all names. He is exercising dominion and authority over all things. The Lamb who was slain for the world is now the Lion who reigns as King.

The ascension of Christ reminds us that the One who was wounded, the One who endured suffering, the One who bore our sin to the point of death, is alive and exalted. He knows our frame. He knows our weaknesses. He knows our temptations. He willingly partook of our human experience. And He is reigning now, at this very moment, not as an earthly monarch who is insensible to the plight of His subjects, but as our Savior-King who condescended to our state.

The fullness of the gospel of King Jesus is seen not just at the cross but from cradle to coronation. His incarnation, sinless life, death, resurrection, and ascension show us that the Son has indeed accomplished our salvation. Consider the magnificent sweep of what He has accomplished for us:

> In Christ, you are *forgiven* (Acts 5:31).
>
> In Christ, you are *saved* (2 Tim. 1:9; Titus 3:5).
>
> In Christ, you are *justified* (Gal. 2:16).
>
> In Christ, you are *reconciled* (Rom. 5:11).
>
> In Christ, you are *loved* (1 John 3:16).
>
> In Christ, you are *adopted* (Gal. 4:5).
>
> In Christ, you are *cleansed* (Acts 15:9; Eph. 5:26).
>
> In Christ, you are *healed* (1 Pet. 2:24).
>
> In Christ, you are *redeemed* (Heb. 9:15; Gal. 3:13).
>
> In Christ, you are *free* (Rev. 1:5).
>
> In Christ, you are *rescued* (Gal. 1:4).
>
> In Christ, you are *triumphant* (Col. 2:15).
>
> In Christ, you have *hope* (Col. 1:27).
>
> In Christ, you have an *inheritance* (1 Pet. 1:4).
>
> In Christ, you have *peace* (Col. 1:20).
>
> In Christ, you have *rest* (Heb. 4:3).

The fullness of our understanding of salvation grows when we meditate on these truths. They are like facets in the diamond that is our redemption, each enhancing the preciousness of that costly gift. With such a catalog of grace, let it never be said that Christians ran short in speech to describe how great a salvation we have received in Christ.

Maybe this is the first time you've connected the theological realities that we've discussed in the past few chapters. God made everything, including you. He is good and He is King. He made you with divine dignity to reign and rule on His behalf in order to accomplish His purposes in the world. But instead of living as God's image-bearers, we've rebelled against Him—each and every one of us. But God, being rich in mercy, doesn't abandon us to death and despair. He is the God who, in His deep love for us, came to rescue us—He came to rescue you. He has come to cleanse, forgive, and welcome His children back home. He doesn't invite us back into His kingdom as a servant. He invites us back into His kingdom as sons and daughters—as coheirs with Christ. All because of what Jesus Christ has accomplished for us. We hope you believe that. If you haven't yet, we hope you will now, by praying to God thanking Him for what He has given you in Christ.

Redeemed. Rescued. A costly deliverance from a certain death. We are not so different from those imperiled lives trembling in a dark cave in Thailand, brought safely out. Christ the King has led us out in triumphal procession. God has "rescued us from the domain of darkness and transferred us into the kingdom of the Son he loves. In him we have redemption, the forgiveness of sins" (Col. 1:13–14). All hail King Jesus.

You Are a Theologian

Discuss

1. How balanced is your conception of the dual nature of Christ? Which nature do you tend to emphasize over the other—divine or human? Why do you think your emphasis tends to lie in that direction?

2. How does Jesus's life of perfect obedience help you understand the good news of the gospel better? How does it call you to follow His example? Specifically, what sin do you need to confess and turn from?

3. How should the resurrection of Christ impact the way believers look toward their own deaths? How does it speak to our fears about death and dying?

4. How does the ascension address our anxieties when we feel life is out of control? What current anxiety would be reduced for you if you meditated on the reality of Christ's current reign and rule of all things?

5. Look back through the list of Christ's accomplishments on your behalf. Which one is hardest for you to believe is true about you? Memorize the Scripture reference so that you can meditate on the glorious truth(s) about who you are in Christ.

Pray

Read this prayer from church father, Gregory of Nazianzus, and meditate on the person and work of Jesus. Underline the words that stand out to you as you read. Then read the prayer aloud, beginning each line with, "Father, thank You that . . ."

> He hungered—but He fed thousands.
>
> He was wearied, but He is the Rest of them that are weary.
>
> He was heavy with sleep, but He walked lightly over the sea.
>
> He prays, but He hears prayer.
>
> He weeps, but He causes tears to cease.
>
> He asks where Lazarus was laid, for He was man; but He raises Lazarus, for He was God.
>
> He is sold, and very cheap, for it is only thirty pieces of silver; but He redeems the world.

As a sheep He is led to the slaughter, but He
is the Shepherd of Israel,and now of the
whole world also.

As a lamb He is silent, yet He is the Word.

He is wounded, but He heals every disease.

He dies, but He gives life.

CHAPTER 8

What Has God Done?
(Part 2)

Pneumatology: The Doctrine
of the Holy Spirit

Brief Definition: *The Holy Spirit is sent by the Father and the Son to apply the saving accomplishments of Christ to believers. The Spirit applies salvation by granting faith, uniting us to Christ, while sanctifying, persevering, and glorifying all followers of Christ.*

Among the characters found in great literature, perhaps no character is more likely to have been misunderstood or overlooked than Arthur Radley. He haunts the pages of one of the most famous novels in American literature, Harper

Lee's *To Kill a Mockingbird*, a novel most of us were forced to read at a stage of life during which we were least likely to absorb its layered beauties. But if you allow yourself to revisit the story for pleasure rather than for a grade in high school English class, Arthur will be there waiting for you, waiting to be remembered—or perhaps discovered with adult eyes.

In the story, he is referred to not by his given name but by the nickname "Boo Radley." He is the shadowy figure who lives next door to the main character, a young girl named Scout. In the course of the novel, Scout moves from not knowing Arthur exists, to being terrified of his existence, to learning that he has been a protective presence for her all along.

Of the three persons of the Trinity, none is more apt to be misunderstood or forgotten than the Third Person, the Holy Spirit. Like Scout's relationship to Boo Radley, we may simply overlook Him or avoid Him out of fear or confusion. We will make it our goal in this chapter to reclaim the Spirit's place in the godhead, to return Him to full personhood, and to remind ourselves of His work in the world and in our lives. But first, let's review the actions of each member of the Trinity we introduced in chapter 2: God the Father *initiates* all divine activity. He sends God the Son to *accomplish* our salvation. The Father and the Son send the Spirit to *apply* our salvation. God the Father initiates, God the Son accomplishes, God the Spirit applies. All that the Father wills, all that Christ purchases, is given to us through the Spirit of God. In this chapter, we will explore who the Holy Spirit is and what He does in His work of application.

Not only has God come to rescue us in Christ, but God continues to save His people through the Holy Spirit. For the believer, salvation is ongoing in the sense that those delivered from sin's penalty (justification) now experience deliverance from sin's power (sanctification), and will one day be delivered from sin's presence (glorification). The Spirit is active in each of these aspects of salvation.

We call the study of the Holy Spirit *pneumatology*, from the Greek word *pneuma*, meaning "breath" or "spirit." You will recall from chapter 2 that God eternally exists as one God in three distinct persons—God the Father, God the Son, and God the Holy Spirit—each of whom is fully God, yet there is one God. We have considered the work of the Son in our salvation—who He is and what He does. But who exactly is the Holy Spirit, and what does He do?

Five Misconceptions about the Holy Spirit

Before we look at His attributes and work, let's dismiss five of the most common misconceptions about Him:

1. *The Holy Spirit Is a Force.*

The Spirit is sometimes conceived of almost like a super-power Christians invoke when they are in need of help or an emotional lift. Rather than a person, He is seen as an impersonal force. This essentially commodifies God, in much the same way we are prone to commodify our neighbors. We tend to value those in helping roles only for the help they offer, and the same can be true of the way we think of the Spirit. We conceive of Him as a button to push for service, rather than as a person to love and worship. He is not a force or a power, though He can be forceful and powerful. He is a person. He is fully God and worthy of honor, adoration, worship, and praise.

2. *The Holy Spirit Comes and Goes.*

It is common to hear Christians invite the Spirit to descend or to blow through a room. It is also common to hear people express that they feel God is far off. It is true that we hear scriptural accounts of the Spirit descending on someone or departing from someone, but these accounts speak of a particular work of the Spirit. They are not describing the indwelling of the Spirit that all believers receive, but a nonnormative work. When we receive the Spirit at our conversion, He is always in us—even when we don't feel His presence or act like someone indwelt with the Spirit. He is also omnipresent, everywhere fully present, though we may not perceive Him to be.

3. *The Holy Spirit Is an Emotion or Feeling.*

Got goose bumps? That's the Spirit's presence. Missing goose bumps? No Spirit detected. In our understanding, the Holy Spirit is often tied to the way we feel. We describe certain praise music, prayers, or worship services as "Spirit-filled" and others as average or boring. Many would say the Spirit speaks to them through Psalm 23, but fewer would say He speaks to them through the dietary laws of Leviticus. Yet, all Scripture is God-breathed. We say, "I am praying for peace about this decision," as though the Spirit gives peace before we should act. But the Bible says we know the good we ought to do and we still don't do it (James 4:17). In other words, sometimes we need to do the right thing whether our liver quivers or not. Our feelings matter, but they are not necessarily reliable indicators of the Spirit's presence or work. The Spirit is not a feeling—He's a person!

4. *The Holy Spirit Is Dramatic.*

Signs and wonders, healings, dramatic conversions, deliverance from addictions or life-threatening circumstances—we

YOU ARE A THEOLOGIAN

are not wrong to associate these with the Holy Spirit. They are certainly so. But if we only associate the dramatic with the Spirit, we do Him an injustice. If we only celebrate our pastor for showing up big at weddings, funerals, and baptisms but fail to recognize his steady, faithful presence in matters big and small, we diminish the credit he is due. Similarly, those who love the Spirit as a person recognize His activity and sustaining care in the everyday as well as in the extraordinary.

5. The Holy Spirit Is Nice, but Not Necessary.

A common response to an overly dramatized view of the Spirit is to downplay His role. It is sometimes joked that the functional Trinity of many churches is the Father, the Son, and the Holy Bible. The implicit assumption is that Scripture is all the pneuma we need. But, while it is important to uphold the work of the Spirit through Scripture, we must also uphold His very real presence and work in our hearts and minds and lives on a daily basis. He is the Helper without whom we would not be able to retain our justification, and without whom we would not be able to effect our sanctification. It is not only His words that we need, but His activity. He is essential to our lives. He, the Spirit, is essential to life and godliness!

The Spirit Is Eternal,
Omnipresent, God Himself

How, then, should we think of the Holy Spirit? The fourth-century Nicene Creed points us toward some key ideas to help shape our understanding:

> We believe in the Holy Spirit, the Lord, the giver of life, who proceeds from the Father and the Son. With the Father and the Son He is worshipped and glorified. He has spoken through the Prophets.[9]

Note the reference to the God-breathed words of the prophets. As we saw in chapter 3, the Spirit breathed out the Scriptures through human authors. Note also the reference to the Spirit as the giver of life. The Spirit hovers over the chaotic waters at creation, waiting to breathe out life, and also signifying His eternality (Gen. 1:2).

The Nicene Creed takes care to describe the Holy Spirit not as a force, but as a person, fully God: "The Lord . . . [who] with the Father and Son . . . is worshipped and glorified." As we noted in chapter 2, the Bible gives ample indication the Spirit is indeed God Himself. Writing to the Corinthians, Paul argues for the distinct personhood and divinity of the Spirit: "For who knows a person's thoughts except his spirit within him? In the same way, no one knows the thoughts of God except the Spirit of God" (1 Cor. 2:11).

In one of the most shocking scenes in the book of Acts, Ananias and Sapphira lie about the sale of a piece of land. Peter responds, "Why has Satan filled your heart to lie to the Holy Spirit and keep back part of the proceeds of the land? . . . You have not lied to people but to God" (Acts 5:3–4). The personhood of the Holy Spirit can be seen in the nature of the offense: you have not lied to people, but to the Person of the Spirit. We have every reason to believe we are capable of doing the same. Any attempt to deceive another person is ultimately an attempt to deceive God Himself.

The Spirit Proceeds

Since the Holy Spirit is God, what distinguishes Him from the Father and Son? The Nicene Creed helps by telling us He proceeds from the Father and the Son. But what does that mean? Simply that the Spirit is eternally sent by the Father and Son to apply the accomplishments of salvation.

In the Upper Room Discourse in John's Gospel, Jesus teaches His disciples about the distinct procession of the Holy Spirit. He indicates He is going to leave them but the Spirit is going to come to them and be their Helper: "But the Counselor, the Holy Spirit, whom the Father will send in my name, will teach you all things and remind you of everything

I have told you" (John 14:26). He continues, "When the Counselor comes, the one I will send to you from the Father—the Spirit of truth who proceeds from the Father—he will testify about me" (John 15:26). And then, in John 16:7 He makes this jaw-dropping statement: "It is for your benefit that I go away, because if I don't go away the Counselor will not come to you. If I go, I will send him to you." Jesus comforts His disciples by telling them the Holy Spirit's presence with them is *better than* His own presence with them. But how can this be? Because the Holy Spirit is not just God *with* us but God *in* us.

After His resurrection, and immediately before His ascension, one of Jesus's first actions is to breathe out the Holy Spirit on His disciples. "He breathed on them and said, "Receive the Holy Spirit" (John 20:22). He shows that not only is He the God who creates but, the God who recreates. The indwelling of the Holy Spirit is not only true for those disciples who were present with Jesus at His resurrection; it is true for anybody who would follow Jesus. Immediately after His ascension, Jesus does the same thing for all disciples. At Pentecost we see that anybody who believes in Jesus through faith receives the Spirit of God.

Peter preaches the gospel, and the crowd responds by asking, "What are we supposed to do?" Peter answers, "Repent and be baptized, each of you, in the name of Jesus Christ for the forgiveness of your sins, and you will receive the gift of the

Holy Spirit" (Acts 2:38). When we receive the good news of the gospel through faith, we don't just receive forgiveness of sins we receive the very presence of God. Not only does the Spirit of God breathe life into humanity formed from the dirt, but He also breathes life into humanity reborn in the gospel.

And that is exactly what we need. We don't just need God to be with us, or God to be for us—though we need those things too. We need God to be *in* us, so that the work of Christ can be applied to us.

This is why the Father and the Son send the Spirit, in order to apply the accomplishments of Christ—to make His accomplishments ours. What Christ secured, the Spirit gives. Those Christ has justified, the Spirit enlivens, unites to Christ, sanctifies, preserves, and glorifies. The Spirit makes us coheirs in the kingdom of Christ. He gives us the King and the kingdom.

Accomplishments Applied: Regeneration

The Spirit takes everything that is made ours in Christ, and He gives it to us. He does this first by enlivening us, or giving us new life (John 6:63). Theologians call this the doctrine of *regeneration*—being born again. We are familiar with the term "born-again Christian," but consider where it comes from and how it points to the work of the Spirit in our justification.

In John 3, a teacher of the law named Nicodemus comes to Jesus and questions His spiritual authority, wondering how He is able to perform signs and miracles. Jesus tells him: "Truly I tell you, unless someone is born again, he cannot see the kingdom of God" (John 3:3). This whole category of being born again is new to Nicodemus. He wants to know what to do. He wants to know how to improve himself—morally, ethically, religiously. He wants to know what he can do to assure himself of inheriting the kingdom.

But Jesus makes it abundantly clear that our greatest need is not renovation, but rebirth. We need to be born of the Spirit. Inheriting the kingdom of God is not about what *we* do, but about what *God* does in us. The first work of the Holy Spirit is not to give us a list of dos and don'ts but to make us alive again.

Jesus continues, "Unless someone is born of water and the Spirit, he cannot enter the kingdom of God. Whatever is born of the flesh is flesh, and whatever is born of the Spirit is spirit" (John 3:5–6). This is Jesus's way of saying we cannot receive the kingdom through our activity, but only through grace. The kingdom is not inherited through flesh, but through the Spirit.

Jesus reiterates His point by telling Nicodemus this is not something humans can do on their own. Nobody decides to be born, and nobody decides to be born again. Rather, the work of the Spirit is like wind, Jesus teaches. It can't be created; it can only be received. It can't even be predicted, only witnessed. Jesus teaches Nicodemus, "The wind blows where it pleases, and you hear its sound, but you don't know where it comes from or where it is going. So it is with everyone born of the Spirit" (John 3:8).

Our dead hearts need revival, and the Spirit brings it. The work of the Spirit is not created or manipulated; it can only be received in faith. The only way to receive the accomplishments of Christ is through faith. Faith is not simply a matter of human ability. It's not only a matter of intellect. Faith is a gift. Paul tells the Ephesians, "For you are saved by grace through faith, and this is not from yourselves; it is God's gift—not from works, so that no one can boast" (Eph. 2:8–9). And Paul should know. He was granted the gracious gift of faith like a lightning bolt from the heavens on a road to Damascus. Every radical conversion story attests to the gracious gift of faith, but so also do the less dramatic ones if we take the time to examine them. Salvation is a gift of grace and the work of the Spirit from beginning to end. The Spirit regenerates us, applying Christ's justifying work to our spirits. But that's not all.

Accomplishments Applied: United to Christ

All that is in Christ is now ours through the Spirit. As we discussed in the last chapter, the word *for* helps us understand

Christ's work. Christ died *for* sinners. In the same way, the word *in* helps us understand the Spirit's work in applying salvation. The Spirit places us *in* Christ and Christ *in* us. Sin unites us to Adam, but the Spirit unites us to Christ (Rom. 5).

Paul regularly employs that seemingly insignificant preposition *in* to communicate the enormous effects of the gospel. The Bible asserts that the presence of the Spirit in the believer makes us forever inseparable from Christ and His benefits. We are *in* Him, and He is *in* us. Christ cannot deny Himself, so He can never deny us.

One of the clearest places the Bible teaches this is in Paul's letter to the Romans. In his discussion of the believer's new relationship to sin, he emphasizes our new union with Christ:

> Or are you unaware that all of us who were baptized into Christ Jesus were baptized into his death? Therefore we were buried with him by baptism into death, in order that, just as Christ was raised from the dead by the glory of the Father, so we too may walk in newness of life. For if we have been united with him *in* the likeness of his death, we will certainly also be *in* the likeness of his resurrection. (Rom. 6:3–5, emphasis added)

The life of the believer is forever united to the life of Christ. His life is ours. His death is ours. His resurrection is ours. His future is ours. His love from the Father is now ours.

How is union with Christ applied to and assured for the believer? Paul tells us:

> In [Christ] you also were sealed with the promised Holy Spirit when you heard the word of truth, the gospel of your salvation, and when you believed. The Holy Spirit is the down payment of our inheritance, until the redemption of the possession, to the praise of his glory. (Eph. 1:13–14)

The Spirit seals us with Christ with a seal that cannot be broken. When the Spirit unites you to Christ, your life becomes completely and utterly inseparable from Christ. He is yours and you are His. For those battling assurance of their salvation, for those doubting they have truly been reconciled to God, recall that you are sealed by the Spirit with an unbreakable seal. You are in Christ. You are secure not just because of what Christ did *for* you but also because His Spirit lives *in* you. But that's not all.

Christ's Accomplishments
Applied: Sanctification

Not only are we sealed by the Spirit in union with Christ, we are also being made holy. In Christ, God has come to fight *for* us. In the Spirit, God has come to fight *in* us, waging war against ungodliness (Col. 3:5). The Spirit's work of new life in the believer leads us to repent of our former way of life. Repentance means a turn from one thing to another. This turning is marked by a profound change in our desires. When we are made alive in the Spirit, we begin to lose our old desire for sin, and we begin to develop a new desire for Christ (Acts 2:38).

When we are made alive, we no longer bend inexorably toward unrighteousness, but instead we bend toward righteousness. Our new birth does not make us immediately perfect, but we are granted new affections. We learn to desire what is good and hate what is evil. We know that through justification we have been declared holy, but in sanctification, the Holy Spirit empowers us to actual, personal godliness. Put another way, those who receive positional holiness at the cross live lives of practical holiness hereafter by the Spirit.

Obedience does not have to wait for the kingdom to come; we are empowered by the Spirit to obey the King now. If we are truly in Christ, then He is not *just* our justification, but He is also our sanctification. Since His Spirit is now alive

153

in the believer, He enables us to live in righteousness. We do not live holy lives because we are under the law but because we are under grace and full of the Spirit (Gal. 3:23–26). We don't obey God to earn His love but because we already have it. He has already poured His love into our hearts by His Spirit (Rom. 5:5). We are not just imputed with righteousness; we are renewed to righteous living.

All true faith in Christ, because of the Spirit's work in believers, results in good works for the glory of God. Those to whom the Spirit applies justification, He also empowers for sanctification. Sanctification is not instantaneous or easy. Rather, it is progressive, effort laden, and much slower than we would like. In this life we will not reach perfection. But while we reject the false gospel of perfectionism, we also reject the false gospel of defeatism. We are not perfect. Nor has sin defeated us. We follow the perfect one who grants us obedience. And our Helper dwells within us to guide us in paths of righteousness. But that's not all.

Accomplishments Applied: Perseverance and Glorification

The Spirit also preserves Christians to the end. Those who belong to Christ in the Spirit cannot be lost. This glorious truth is the doctrine of perseverance. The Bible admonishes all believers to persevere to the end (Rom. 2:7–8). Yet

Christians are warned of threats on every side, and we all have stories in our lives of people who have fallen away. So, can the grace that has been started in us fail to be completed in us?

If perseverance in the faith was up to you, you would not make it. You would fall short. But with the Spirit at work in Christians, all that the Father has given the Son will come to Him. No one shall pluck us out of His hand (John 6:37; 10:28). The God who saves His people is the same God who keeps His people—all the way to the end. The good down payment of the Holy Spirit will carry us to glory. The Spirit will see us through the tribulation of this life, aiding us in our battle against sin, and the Spirit will usher us into glory, where we will beat our swords into plowshares, and the battle will be won.

There is great comfort in the Christian life. We have assurance of salvation not because of our works, not because of our spiritual performance, but because we are sealed forever and kept forever by the Spirit. We will persevere because He will preserve us.

In the wake of all that is wretched and wrecked in this world of sin and sorrow, see how the triune God has come to our rescue.

> What has gone wrong in the world? Sin.
> What has God done?
> God the Father sent the Son.
> God the Son accomplished salvation.
> God the Spirit applies salvation.

No Small Miracle

So go ahead and associate the Third Person of the Trinity with signs and wonders. What a miraculous work of the Spirit is regeneration, the enlivening of faith in a heart of stone! What an astonishing miracle that our Helper can train our desires toward righteousness, that our obedience would clearly identify us as the children of God! What sign is more potent, what wonder is greater than a life marked by persevering submission to God by the power of our Comforter, the Spirit. The wonderful works of our salvation are worthy of every emotion they stir, every goose bump they produce. And the Person who applies them, eternally proceeding from the Father and the Son, is worthy of our worship.

You Are a Theologian

Discuss

1. Look back at the five common misconceptions about the Holy Spirit. Which of them have you held personally? Which does your church hold? How has this chapter challenged your perspective on the identity and role of the Spirit?

2. How does the concept of union with Christ offer you personal and specific assurance? What past or present sin do you

doubt He can forgive? What past, present, or future circumstance do you fear could tear you from His grip?

3. How have you seen the Spirit at work in your sanctification? How has the Spirit functioned as a Helper and Counselor?

4. How have you known the Spirit as the preserver of your salvation? What doubts can you lay to rest knowing you are sealed in Him and that He stands as the guarantee that you will be glorified?

Pray

Below is Augustine's Prayer to the Holy Spirit. Meditate on each line, adding specific requests for your own thoughts, work, loves, and battles in the margin. Then pray Augustine's prayer aloud, adding your personal requests.

> *Breathe into me, Holy Spirit,*
> *that my thoughts may all be holy.*

> *Move in me, Holy Spirit,*
> *that my work, too, may be holy.*

> *Attract my heart, Holy Spirit,*
> *that I may love only what is holy.*

> *Strengthen me, Holy Spirit,*
> *that I may defend all that is holy.*

Protect me, Holy Spirit,
that I may always be holy.

—Augustine of Hippo (354–430 CE)

CHAPTER 9

To Whom Do We Belong?

Ecclesiology: The Doctrine of the Church

Brief Definition: *The church is the family of God that is created by the Father through the Word, led by the Son, and filled with the Spirit. It is universal, local, and celebratory.*

In 1965, a music-filled family sang its way into the hearts of Americans, and it never left. The movie *The Sound of Music* released to wide acclaim and multiple awards. It became the highest grossing film in history, maintaining that honor for five consecutive years, and its worldwide popularity remains today, establishing it as an enduring movie classic. *The Sound of Music* offered more than just a catchy musical score; it offered a compelling story. It is a story of a woman with no family who finds one that would not be complete without her. It is a story about belonging, commitment, and shared belief and purpose. It speaks to anyone who has ever known loneliness and longed to belong.

Like all great stories, *The Sound of Music* endures in its appeal because it is not telling a new story, but an old one. And a true one. The Bible speaks of the value and necessity of belonging, commitment, and shared belief and purpose. In recent years, evangelistic messages have emphasized an invitation to a personal relationship with Jesus Christ. No doubt, in our individualistic culture, this message has a certain appeal. But just as the story of Maria Von Trapp finds its beauty in the individual as part of a family, so does the story of our salvation. Christian, here is good news: there is no such thing as "you in a personal relationship with Jesus Christ." To be a believer is to be in relationship with both God and His church.

We call the study of the church *ecclesiology*, from the Greek word *ekklesia*, meaning "gathering" or "assembly." The doctrine of salvation declares the good news that we belong to God. The doctrine of the church declares the good news that we belong to one another. In an age of individualism, the call to belong is both countercultural and compelling. "Christian individualism" is an oxymoron. We are called not just to believe in the church, but to belong to it—both the church universal and the church local.

The universal church is made up of all believers, of all times and all locations. The church universal stretches *outward* to every nation, tribe, and tongue, *backward* through time to all previous generations of believers, and *forward* to all future generations of believers. John's vision in Revelation shows us a snapshot of the church universal, where every nation, tribe, and tongue worships before the throne of God. The universal church reminds believers of the beauty of our fundamental unity in Christ, no matter our particular context.

The local church is the embodied gathering of Christians in a particular time and place, centered around the proclamation of the Word and celebration of the ordinances (more on that in a bit). These local churches may speak different languages, believe slightly differently on secondary issues, and express worship through varying styles, each seeking to make the glory of God known where they are, each in their particular context. The local church reminds believers of the beauty of diversity that exists among the children of God.

We will return to a discussion of the local church later in this chapter, but let's begin by expanding our understanding of the church in general terms. The New Testament gives us multiple metaphors to teach us about the nature and function of the church. It asks us to consider the church as a family, a temple, a priesthood, a stranger, a body, and a bride. These metaphors have application for both the church universal (the church across the ages) and the church local (your church in your particular context).

The Church Is a Family

In the previous chapter, we saw Pentecost as the day the Spirit was breathed into the people of God. Because the Spirit is in every Christian, we are united not only with Christ, but also to one another. Pentecost marks the birth of the church, and like the new birth each of us experiences in Christ, the church does not decide to be born. It is birthed by the Father through the Word. The church comes into being through the proclamation of the gospel when the Father and Son pour out the Spirit in order to bring about a new sort of family. The church does not make itself come into being—Christ, the head of the church, brings it into being by making dead people come alive through His Word (Acts 2).

Jesus speaks of the new sort of family that is formed in our salvation. One day as He is teaching, He is interrupted and told that His mother and brothers are waiting to speak to Him. He seizes the opportunity to instruct those listening:

> He replied to him, "Who is my mother, and
> who are my brothers?" Pointing to his disci-
> ples, he said, "Here are my mother and my
> brothers. For whoever does the will of my

Father in heaven is my brother and sister and
mother." (Matt. 12:48–50 NIV)

Jesus is not minimizing the significance of our literal
family connections. Rather, He is expanding our understanding of the significance of our spiritual family. When we are
adopted by God through Christ, we become a part of God's
family. This is good news in the extreme. No matter our family of origin or marital status, no matter whether we are an
only child or a child of many siblings, no matter whether
we are a parent or not, no matter whether we were loved or
neglected by our earthly parents, no matter if we are single,
married, divorced, widowed, infertile, young, old, rich, poor,
Jew or Gentile, male or female—all Christians belong to
God's family.

Consider the metaphor of church as family. This family
is marked by love for one another. Brotherly and sisterly love
is meant to permeate all church families, as the command to
love one another is one of the most consistent commands to
the church in the New Testament. In fact, there is no such
thing as a Christian who does not exhibit brotherly love:
"The one who loves God must also love his brother and sister" (1 John 4:21).

In the midst of cultural ache and personal pain around
loneliness, alienation, and isolation, the church is meant
to be a redemptive remedy. In the church we are meant to

experience a sacred siblinghood and shared sense of mission that all of us long for.

The Church Is a Temple

Family is not the only metaphor that the new Testament gives to the church. Paul reminds the Corinthian church,

> Do you not know that *you* are God's temple and that God's Spirit dwells in *you*? If anyone destroys God's temple, God will destroy him. For God's temple is holy, and *you* are that temple. (1 Cor. 3:16–17 ESV, emphasis added)

Do you read Paul's words here and think of yourself, the individual, as God's temple? In 1 Corinthians 6, Paul will indeed address the individual along similar lines, but here he is making a broader argument. He is speaking of the church.

Theologian, and Texan, John Dyer has noted the trend to read passages individualistically, and the problem with doing so. Almost forty-eight hundred verses in the Bible contain the English word "you," but no distinction is made between the singular or the plural usage in the original language. To help with the problem, Dyer created a plug-in that converts the original second-person plural usages from "you" to "y'all." He called it, magnificently, the Texas Bible Plug-in.[10] Now read

Paul's words with the plural restored (Texas style), and note the difference in emphasis:

> Do you not know that *y'all* are God's temple
> and that God's Spirit dwells in *y'all*? If anyone
> destroys God's temple, God will destroy him.
> For God's temple is holy, and *y'all* are that
> temple.

Paul is describing not you, the individual, but us, the collective body of believers. We, the church, are God's temple, having received the Spirit collectively at Pentecost. Peter points to temple imagery, as well, when he describes believers as living stones being built up as a spiritual house (1 Pet. 2:5). The same Spirit that blew life through the garden temple of Eden, the same Spirit that blew life through the Old Testament tabernacle and temple, that same Spirit breathes life through the church.

This is the essence of the statement Jesus makes to the woman at the well when she asks a question about the proper location for worship: "An hour is coming, and is now here, when the true worshipers will worship the Father in Spirit and in truth" (John 4:23). Instead of going to a tabernacle or a temple to experience the presence of God, the church is now indwelt by the Spirit and enjoys, in a special sense, the presence and care of God in the world.

The Church Is a Priesthood

The apostle Peter points us to another powerful metaphor for the church, drawing on God's promise to Israel in the Old Testament. At the foot of Sinai, God tells Israel freshly delivered from Egypt, "You will be my kingdom of priests and my holy nation" (Exod. 19:6). With the coming of Christ, the Spirit begins the fulfillment of this promise in the New Testament church. Peter refers to the church as those who are, "being built to be a holy priesthood to offer spiritual sacrifices acceptable to God through Jesus Christ" (1 Pet. 2:5). The church is set apart by God to offer spiritual sacrifices for His glory.

Rather than only a handful of people set aside for special service to God, all believers are given that precious privilege and sacred duty. All men, all women, all children and elderly, every nation, tribe, and tongue. What kinds of sacrifices do we offer? According to Paul, our whole selves: "Therefore, brothers and sisters, in view of the mercies of God, I urge you to present your bodies as a living sacrifice, holy and pleasing to God; this is your true worship" (Rom. 12:1). Put another way, we love God with heart, soul, mind, and strength in everything we think, say, and do.

In Revelation, we see that He who began a good work in His church will be faithful to complete it. The four living creatures and the twenty-four elders proclaim that the

Lamb is worthy of worship, because "you *have made them* to be a kingdom and priests to serve our God" (Rev. 5:10 NIV, emphasis added).

The Church Is a Stranger

Peter also takes care to remind the church of its status as elect exiles, aliens and strangers, sojourners on the way to our true home (1 Pet. 1:1; 2:11). We understand ourselves to be passing through, versus putting down roots. Peter is alluding to the exile of Israel in the Old Testament, and to the example of Abraham, Isaac, and Jacob who lived their entire lives as tent-dwellers, awaiting the fulfillment of God's promise (Heb. 11:9–10).

The testimony of the exile is one of delayed gratification, and so must it be for the church. We must be good at waiting. We should not expect this world to help us get comfortable. Rather, we should expect to be treated as outsiders because we look like outsiders. We must lift our eyes to a coming city. Like Abraham the sojourner, we are "looking forward to the city that has foundations, whose architect and builder is God" (Heb. 11:10). And one day, that city will descend, and the dwelling place of God will be with man (Rev. 21:3).

Until that day, this world will feel hostile to the church of Jesus Christ. But when we feel most like sojourners, we can know with certainty that we belong to God. And to one another. How much sweeter is the journey through a strange land when it is shared by those with the same hope and the same Spirit!

The Church Is a Body

To help us understand our interconnectedness and interdependence, as well as our individual contributions, Paul describes the church as the body of Christ. The New Testament teaches us that we all belong to one another, as one body, but we each have individual functions. Stressing the unity and diversity of the church, Paul tells the Corinthians, "We who are many are one body" (1 Cor. 10:17). A physical body is made of many parts that work together, enlivened by one spirit. So also, the church is made of many different kinds of people with varying gifts, all enlivened by the Spirit of God. Our differences are strengths, not liabilities, and competition and favoritism should have no place in the church.

But the metaphor of a body helps us in another way by pointing us to our witness: as Christ's body in the incarnation made it possible for Him to act as a physical representative of God, so also the church is the physical representation of God in the world today, living sacrificially after the pattern of Christ. The church, then, should have feet that are swift to bring the good news of the gospel, hands that are swift to serve the poor and the outcast, words that are swift to encourage and exhort the weary and downtrodden, and prayers that are swift to intercede for the spiritually destitute.

The metaphor of a body also helps us to know our relative importance. Paul tells us in Ephesians 1:22–23 that the body, which is the church, has a head, and that head is Christ. By this, we understand that we are not in charge. We submit ourselves to our head, seeking to live as He commands us. The desires of the individual bow to the desires of the whole. The desires of the whole align with the desires of the head. We say along with Paul, "Let us grow in every way into him who is the head—Christ. From him the whole body, fitted and knit together by every supporting ligament, promotes the growth of the body for building itself up in love by the proper working of each individual part" (Eph. 4:15–16).

The Church Is a Bride

Finally, we are given the metaphor of the church as a bride. Paul compares the marriage of a husband and wife to Christ's marriage to His bride, the church: "This mystery is profound, but I am talking about Christ and the church" (Eph. 5:32). Paul shows the church is now knit together with Christ in an unbreakable union. In the Old Testament, Israel was depicted metaphorically as a wife, albeit an unfaithful one. The church is spoken of as a betrothed bride who is to be presented without blemish on her wedding day.

YOU ARE A THEOLOGIAN

Paul speaks of his desire to see the church remain pure in her betrothal: "For I am jealous for you with a godly jealousy, because I have promised you in marriage to one husband— to present a pure virgin to Christ" (2 Cor. 11:2). When the church understands itself to be a bride in waiting, purity becomes paramount. Holiness becomes of utmost concern. As we noted in the chapter on the Holy Spirit, positional holiness is ours in Christ, but practical holiness is the task of the bride as she awaits her Bridegroom.

Once again, the concept of waiting features into our understanding of the role of the church. The book of Revelation speaks of the marriage supper of the Lamb:

> Hallelujah, because our Lord God, the
>   Almighty, reigns!
> Let us be glad, rejoice, and give him glory,
>   because the marriage of the Lamb has
>   come,
> and his bride has prepared herself.
> She was given fine linen to wear, bright and
>   pure.
> For the fine linen represents the righteous
>   acts of the saints. (Rev. 19:6–8)

Note that "his bride *has prepared* herself"—the good work He began in His church is completed. Her righteous acts, empowered by the Spirit, have set her apart as holy. The church is a bride awaiting her wedding day, industriously preparing herself by walking in righteousness.

The Local Church: Its Leaders and Practices

Now, let's move from the metaphorical to the practical. Having considered what the church is like, how should the local church function practically? Who leads it? And what are its essential practices? As we noted, the head of the church is Christ (Col. 1:18). In any discussion of who leads the church, we must never forget that Jesus leads His church. Our various traditions are populated with leaders of different titles and roles, but ultimately all church leaders are just under-shepherds, temporary stewards, because the church belongs to Jesus. Jesus is present and active in His church. He distributes the benefits of His salvation through the Word and by His Spirit.

The Bible addresses how churches are to organize themselves but sometimes not to the extent that many wish. This has led to the diversity of different Christian traditions organizing their governing structures in various ways. Some have emphasized centralized authority and others local autonomy. While Christians can disagree about how the church is best governed, at a minimum we can see three simple roles or offices that help the church function.

One office in a local church is that of *elder/shepherd*, which means teacher or leader. This is someone who leads the church through preaching, teaching, protecting the church from false doctrine, and prayer. Jesus raises up these shepherds to oversee and lead local churches (1 Tim. 3; Titus 1; 1 Pet. 5).

A second office in a local church is that of *deacon*, which means servant. Deacons serve the church in various ways by supporting the work of the elders and their leadership (1 Tim. 3:8–13). Ministry is not just preaching and praying; there is also administrative work to be done. The early church learned this lesson in Acts 6:1–6 when members of the church were being neglected in food distribution because of a lack of administrative oversight. Instead of the apostles assuming this burden upon themselves, they appointed servants to care for the daily administrative needs of the church. This enabled the ministry of preaching and prayer to continue and for the church to be cared for administratively.

If you know someone who serves the church in administration, thank them. They are likely a gift to that body. Another way you can serve that church is through faithful giving. The ministry of any local body can only continue through the faithful and sacrificial giving of the body.

Finally, all local churches are made up of *members*. While not technically an office, members are the essence of any local church. Members are the individual believers who are connected to a local body of Christ (Eph. 4:12). This means the members of the church are to gather together for worship of God and celebration of the gospel. Membership at a church is more than just being listed on a membership directory somewhere—it is to be meaningfully connected to a local group of Christians. The Christian life is not meant to be lived in isolation but weekly in the context of the local church.

In an age of dwindling church attendance among professing Christians, we need the reminder of Hebrews 10:24–25: "And let us consider one another in order to provoke love and good works, not neglecting to gather together, as some are in the habit of doing, but encouraging each other, and all the more as you see the day approaching." Gathering together is how we reap the mutual encouragement we need to continue in love and good works. Just as a family that has dinner together regularly is able to maintain a strong family identity that guards against risky behaviors, so also the gathered church strengthens us for the daily fight against sin. The more time we can give to local church participation, the more its formative effects will shape us. The less we give, the more the world around us will dictate the shape and health of our spiritual lives.

But what practices are essential to the local church? Every community has rhythms or rituals that help its members celebrate, learn, and remember who they are. Sociologists and philosophers have called these "social imaginaries" or "symbolic universes," which is a fancy way of saying: rhythms that help a group of people maintain a shared meaning and a shared story. Countries may do this by having special patriotic celebrations that commemorate an important event, like July 4th. Sports teams do this through fight songs and chants. Fitness communities use specific words for workouts and scores. Families develop inside jokes or shared holiday rituals. Every community that desires to stay intact maintains shared rhythms and rituals that help them tell their story, and the church is no different. We, too, have rhythms, given to us by Christ, that help us remember the gospel. Specifically, the local church gathers around the Word and sacrament in order to rehearse the gospel with one another.

The church gathers around the Word because it is the Word of life. Much like the disciples in John 6 when others are abandoning Jesus, we must recognize we have nowhere else to go but to the Word of life. Every local church should organize itself around the proclamation of Scripture in sermons, classes, groups, and curriculum. God's Word is the very lifeblood of the church and the means by which the Spirit builds, edifies, strengthens, and sanctifies the church. The church is a Word-centered community.

In addition to the Word, the church gathers around the sacraments, or ordinances—physical practices that remind us of what Christ has accomplished. Jesus offers the church two primary practices in baptism and the Lord's Supper. These rhythms help us look back in remembrance of what He has done, and to look forward in anticipation of what He will yet do.

Baptism

Baptism is the initial celebration of entering into the family of Christ. Jesus commands His disciples to baptize new family members in the triune name as they proclaim the gospel to the nations (Matt. 28:19). The word *baptize* in the New Testament means to wash ceremonially for the purpose of purification by water. Though important disagreements exist on various modes and candidates for baptism, all Christians agree that baptism marks new family members. It signifies our birth into the family.

God frequently uses water to mark significant events in redemptive history. The Spirit hovering over the waters at creation, the flood, the parting of the Red Sea, and the crossing of the Jordan River are all, in some sense, shadows of the greater reality we have in baptism. Baptism is the practice in which we proclaim that God brings order out of chaos, destroys the enemy of sin, and births new people into His family, and that He will be present with us forever.

In baptism we remember that we have died with Christ, through faith, that our sins have been forgiven, and that we have been washed clean. We testify that the Spirit of God has been poured out on the church and we have been given new life in Christ. Baptism reminds us that God has come to dwell with us in His Spirit and that in the future, we will be resurrected from the grave to dwell with God forever. Baptism reminds us that God is conquering the chaotic forces of the world (Satan, sin, death), subjecting them to judgment, in order to extend His kingdom to all nations. Baptism reminds us that we who have emerged from the water have been crucified with Christ, buried in His death, and raised to walk in new life as sons and daughters of God (Rom. 6:1–4).

The Lord's Supper

In the Lord's Supper we are invited to the family meal. While baptism is the initiation celebration of the church, the Lord's Supper is the ongoing celebration of being kept in the family of God. Not only are we brought into the family, but we are also kept in the family.

As with baptism, important disagreements exist across traditions regarding the practice of the Lord's Supper. But all Christians agree that Jesus initiated this celebration with His disciples in His last meal as one to be continually observed. At the Passover meal just before His crucifixion, He teaches His disciples to remember all that He has accomplished for His brothers and sisters (Matt. 26:26–29). He reimagined the Passover meal of Exodus—the bread His body broken on the cross, the cup of wine His blood shed. And He commands His disciples to eat this meal when they gather, until He returns.

In the Lord's Supper we remember that Jesus's body was crushed and His blood poured out for the forgiveness of sin. In the Lord's Supper, we are not just looking back to the cross, but we are also looking forward to the kingdom. We are anticipating that one day we will enjoy a meal in the kingdom with our King (Rev. 19:6–9).

The Word, baptism, and the Lord's Supper are meant to be intrinsic to the life of the local church, practiced as shared expressions of our faith. In a hyper-individualistic age, these markers of our faith have sometimes been reduced to being primarily or entirely about the experience of the individual, rather than about that individual's connection to the church community. When the church gathers together around the Word and participates in these sacred rhythms, we proclaim the gospel together. We remind ourselves and we announce to the world that this is not our home.

One question we are asked fairly often is, "How do I find a healthy church?" We love this question because we believe regular engagement in the local church is absolutely essential to the spiritual maturity of Christians. In fact, there is no replacement for it.

We acknowledge that there is no perfect church. Every church has its flaws. Sometimes those flaws are fatal. Some churches lose the gospel, lose their authority, and are relegated to spiritual death (Rev. 2).

But other times what is seen to be a flaw is actually just an unrealistic expectation. Especially in an age where we can hear the best preachers online or hop from church to church every few years. What does it look like to find a healthy church and love it the way Jesus does?

When looking for a local church, we would encourage you to think through these kinds of questions:

- Does this church prioritize the good news of Jesus Christ?
- Does this church have a high view of God's Word in preaching and other ministries of the church?
- Does the doctrine of this church align with the historic Christian faith?
- Does the church desire to see me grow, in the context of community, in my love for God and neighbor?
- Does the church regularly observe the ordinances of baptism/Communion?

Looking for a good church can be challenging. But finding one is worth all of the effort. It is a rare and precious gift to know where you belong, to have found a family and a home. The doctrine of the church points us toward that assurance.

Christ has secured for us a family and a home. We belong to one another and to God. We belong with one another and with God. We await a coming King and kingdom, eyes fixed on the horizon, shoulder to shoulder, hand in hand.

You Are a Theologian

Discuss

1. Of the six metaphors offered for the church (family, temple, priesthood, stranger, body, bride), which one is easiest for you to relate to? Which one challenges your understanding of the church the most?

2. How has our culture of individualism impacted your own views of what it means to be a leader or a member in the local church?

3. What feels risky to you about a collective practice of our faith? What feels safe about it? What does being part of something bigger than yourself ask of you and offer to you?

4. What places of belonging are you drawn to that are not the church? Is it wrong to be drawn to belong elsewhere? Why or why not?

Pray

Using each of the metaphors we considered (family, temple, priesthood, stranger, body, bride), write a prayer for your local church. Thank God for every way you see these metaphors being modeled faithfully. Confess to Him where growth could happen. Confess how you have contributed actively or passively to a lesser vision for the church. Boldly ask Him to bring about holiness in His church.

> *Lord, may Your church be a family . . .*
>
> *Lord, may Your church be a temple . . .*
>
> *Lord, may Your church be a priesthood . . .*
>
> *Lord, may Your church be a stranger . . .*
>
> *Lord, may Your church be a body . . .*
>
> *Lord, may Your church be a bride . . .*

CHAPTER 10

How Does the Story End?

Eschatology: The Doctrine of Last Things

Brief Definition: *Our future hope is that Christ will return, raise the dead, execute perfect justice, and establish His kingdom without end. Death does not have the final word.*

Pop quiz: What is the worst movie ever, and why is it *Titanic*? The answer, of course, is because of the way it ends. We all love good stories, and a well-told story builds in us a dissonance that makes us long for a satisfying ending. If the story is well-crafted, the audience will naturally think ahead and ask the question, "How will this all end?" The most enduring stories are those with the most satisfying endings—endings that resolve the dissonance the story has built. We have used stories like these in the writing of this book—children rescued from caves, astronauts safely brought home, tuneful governesses finding happiness and escaping Nazi rule—stories that end well, stories that relieve the tension.

And yet . . . *Titanic*. Come on, James Cameron. Rose and Jack are fictional characters. Fictional! There was no need to (spoiler alert) consign him to a watery grave. Sure, there was no way to spare the ship, or John Jacob Astor IV, but for real? Give the people what they want.

On the subject of satisfying endings, the Bible's story does not disappoint. It is, in fact, the most satisfying ending we could ever hope or imagine. We crave a good ending because we are living in a story that certainly has one, and we feel the dissonance of our place in the plotline.

We live in an age that pervasively ascribes to the depressing and anxiety-inducing belief that there is no overarching story that makes sense of the world. There is no grand story in which to participate. Therefore, our individual stories either terminate on our own happiness or on nothing at all. But the unavoidable (and diabolical) conclusion of an unstoried existence is that our lives are purposeless, aimless, and ultimately meaningless.

Christianity firmly rejects this notion. Purpose, direction, and ultimate meaning are ours in Christ. Stories remind us that we are all living toward something. Meaningful stories make our lives come alive, and we all want to live in a meaningful story. The Christian story, the true story of the world, does just that.

If that's the case, what are we living toward? What is the goal, the *telos*, of the Christian story? The final doctrine we will consider together is the doctrine of end-times, or last things. We call the study of last things *eschatology*, from the Greek word *eschatos*, meaning "last" or "final." The doctrine of eschatology declares the good news that death does not have the final word. The ending to this story is a good one.

A caveat: you can put away your end-times maps and prophecy charts. We are only going to cover the essentials. While convictions abound on secondary matters like the millennium, the tribulation, or the rapture, we have found that sometimes these issues garner so much attention that Christians miss the most important issues contained in eschatology—like the fact that God is coming back to live with His people. As theologian Alistair Begg says, "The main things are the plain things, and the plain things are the main things."[11] While your convictions matter, we will be sticking to the essential "plain things" for the purposes of this discussion.

But what is plain about eschatology? Isn't it all extremely unclear? It's understandable we might feel this way, based on the number of wildly colorful books and movies on the subject. But zoom out and take in the big picture. God would not give us a terrifying or anxiety-inducing vision as the final scene in a story with a very good ending. One of the clearest insights we can gain about eschatology is its purpose. The study of last things is meant primarily for our comfort. Eschatology is primarily meant to encourage the church in the essentials of our future hope, issues like death, the return of Christ, the resurrection from the dead, final judgment, and kingdom without end. End-times meditations are not meant to be anxiety inducing but comfort producing.

Our Comfort in Bodily Death

The doctrine of end times comforts us because it assures us that death is not the end. Death is the great equalizer of humanity. The prophet Isaiah cries:

> "All humanity is grass,
>   and all its goodness is like the flower of the
>   field.
> The grass withers, the flowers fade
> when the breath of the LORD blows on
>   them,
> indeed, the people are grass.
> The grass withers, the flowers fade,
> but the word of our God remains forever."
>   (Isa. 40:6–8)

Grass is a repeated metaphor for humans in the Bible, pointing us to the fleeting nature of our lives and the certainty of our deaths. If we live long enough, we will all experience the loss of someone close to us. And if Jesus does not return in our lifetime, all of us reading this book will one day die, as well.

All humans die because death is the penalty for sin (Rom. 6:23). We inhabit a fallen world, a world of decay, corruption, and death. The Bible describes death as the shroud that covers all people; it is like a sheet that covers all the nations (Isa. 25:7). But what happens when we die?

At death, our material bodies cease to function, but our soul continues to live. Remember, humans are both body and soul. At death, our physical bodies, which are part of who we are, die. Whether our bodies succumb to disease, a fatal accident, or the relentless aging process, we return them to the dust. Ecclesiastes tells us, "All are going to the same place; all come from dust, and all return to dust" (Eccles. 3:20). This is not good news. Our strength, our health, our wealth, our fame, generosity, or humility cannot stop this day from coming. All descendants of Adam return to the dust (Ps. 90:3).

Every death is a tragedy because humans were not made to be put back into the earth, for we were taken from it. Death does not bring about salvation of any kind: it is a reminder of the curse of sin. One of our good friends says, "Let us never call a friend what God calls an enemy." Death is an enemy.

But death's occurrence is not all bad news. It does mark the end of earthly suffering. And for the believer, it marks our entrance into the presence of God. This why Paul can confidently say, "For me to live is Christ, and to die is gain" (Phil. 1:21 ESV). At the moment of death the unity of our body and soul is temporarily separated. While our bodies return to dust, our souls continue to live. At death, believers are immediately ushered into the presence of God, temporarily existing as disembodied souls awaiting the resurrection of the dead.

It is also true that the souls of non-Christians are immediately ushered into torment of judgment and separation from God. They live there as disembodied souls also awaiting resurrection and final judgment. You may be reading this having lost a loved one who was not a believer. This is a hard word, and comfort is difficult to find in it. Perhaps the greatest challenge of our limited knowledge and wisdom as humans is reconciling the goodness of God with our partial and obscured view. While we may be able to give intellectual assent to the goodness of God, our hearts may understandably lag far behind. And the God of infinite compassion looks on us with gentleness in this. He knows we cannot understand what He has done from beginning to end (Eccles. 3:11).

Christians can draw comfort from knowing that our believing loved ones, and we ourselves, are with the Lord at death. Some theologians have called this the beatific vision, which means at death we see God—the most beautiful thing we have ever seen. Paul has such a desire to be with the Lord that he says, "I long to depart and be with Christ—which is far better—but to remain in the flesh is more necessary for your sake" (Phil. 1:23–24). He knows that at the moment of our soul's departure from this world, we are with Christ. We delight in Him and He delights in us. What comfort that is!

Yet, we are also still waiting. Despite the comfort that at death our souls are with the Lord, we are still waiting for the restoration of all things. Paul highlights this struggle:

> For we know that if our earthly tent we live
> in is destroyed, we have a building from God,
> an eternal dwelling in the heavens, not made
> with hands. Indeed, we groan in this tent,
> desiring to put on our heavenly dwelling,
> since, when we are clothed, we will not be
> found naked. Indeed, we groan while we are
> in this tent, burdened as we are, because we
> do not want to be unclothed but clothed, so
> that mortality may be swallowed up by life.
> (2 Cor. 5:1–4)

He describes this intermediate state as one of nakedness, awaiting the clothing of our resurrected bodies that is to come.

The contemplation of the intermediate state is a temporary comfort, because the intermediate state is itself temporary. All people will enter an intermediate state, Christians to bliss, and non-Christians to torment, while we all await the coming of the King. The inevitable nature of death helps us to contemplate our lives, our relationships, and our purpose. Are we living in holiness and virtue? Are we aware of our sin and our need of a Savior? Are we calling others to repent and believe? And do we truly trust that God is good in all His dealings with humans?

Our Comfort in Christ's Return

The doctrine of end-times comforts us because it points us to a King coming back to make everything right. The triumphant return of the ascended Lord to this world is what all of creation is groaning for. Jesus will return visibly, bodily, and suddenly to bring the fullness of salvation to all who are waiting for Him. In Christ's first appearance, He dealt definitively with sin at the cross. In His second appearance, He will bring the fullness of salvation already purchased.

Much ink has been spilled about the precise timing of the return of Christ and the factors or events surrounding His return. But the Bible teaches that no external factors or human manipulation can bring about Christ's return, and that no human calculation can determine its timing. Jesus teaches His disciples, "Now concerning that day or hour no one knows—neither the angels in heaven nor the Son—but only the Father" (Mark 13:32). The time of the coming of

Christ cannot be known, but what *can* be known is it is certainly coming. Until then, we wait.

Waiting implies we are not in control. Only the King builds the kingdom. The citizens of the kingdom simply receive it. Our posture in the meantime is to pray and to wait. As Timothy writes to Titus, "We wait for the blessed hope, the appearing of the glory of our great God and Savior, Jesus Christ" (Titus 2:13).

His appearance will be sudden and definitive, like a thief in the night (1 Thess. 5:2–3). The term that Scripture uses most often to describe this appearance is the Greek word *apocalypse* or its English equivalent, "revelation." Both mean a revealing of something hidden. What we cannot see now, we will see clearly then as Christ brings His kingdom to this world. We are not called to speculate or to pontificate about His return; we are called to watch and to wait.

Paul tells the church that the suddenness of Christ's return should help us to live with sobriety, holiness, and mission (1 Thess. 5). In other words, we ought to live with the end in mind. Christians know where all of world history is heading: toward the return of Christ. Our lives should reflect this reality. The imminent return of Christ is meant to compel all of us to holy lives and missional urgency. Our labor is to live uprightly as aliens and strangers and to proclaim the good news to the ends of the earth.

Our Comfort in Resurrection

The doctrine of end-times comforts us because it tells us our stories end not in death, but in resurrection. Because of the resurrection of Christ, we get to participate in resurrection with Him (Rom. 6:1–4). In God's abundant mercy, Christ's resurrection will one day be our resurrection. His story becomes our story, which means His future is our future. We cannot raise ourselves from the dead, but one day the triune God will raise us from the dead.

The Christian life is lived toward resurrection. The prophet Isaiah comforts us that death will not have the final victory, but God will:

> When he has swallowed up death once and for all, the Lord GOD will wipe away the tears from every face and remove his people's disgrace from the whole earth, for the LORD has spoken. On that day it will be said, "Look, this is our God; we have waited for him, and he has saved us. This is the LORD; we have waited for him. Let's rejoice and be glad in his salvation." (Isa. 25:8–9)

Resurrection is the day we are all longing for. Paul offers a similar note of hope in the face of death by instructing the Corinthian church:

"Death has been swallowed up in victory.
Where, death, is your victory? Where, death,
is your sting?" The sting of death is sin, and
the power of sin is the law. But thanks be to
God, who gives us the victory through our
Lord Jesus Christ! (1 Cor. 15:54–57)

Though death the destroyer was once a burial shroud covering all people, death itself will be destroyed. Those in Christ will trade the shroud of death for the robe of righteousness. One day Christ will have all of the spoils of victory that belong to Him. Our bodies, like seeds in the ground, will one day bear the fruit of the resurrection (1 Cor. 15).

Our future resurrection reminds us of our justification—our names are written in the Book of Life. Our future resurrection fuels our sanctification—the Spirit who will one day raise us from our graves is already at work in us. The doctrine of end-times does not just concern our comfort in the future—it concerns our calling in the present. Today—right now—we want our lives, homes, relationships, and communities to be marked by the future hope we have. We live in the present with an eye toward a glorious future.

Our Comfort in Final Judgment

The doctrine of end-times comforts us because it promises that justice will be served. When Christ returns, He will execute perfect justice. Everything will be made right. It may seem counterintuitive to speak of comfort in the same breath as judgment. Speaking of God's judgment, the author of Hebrews rightly reflects, "It is a terrifying thing to fall into the hands of the living God" (Heb. 10:31). Even as those united with Christ, we know we do not deserve to be spared God's wrath. We remember our former ways. Not only that, but we are familiar with miscarriages of justice at a human level. In a world beset with partiality, weighted scales, and pervasive injustice, our imaginations are seared to the point that we cannot conceive of perfect justice. But that is what makes God's judgment so necessary. There are no weighted scales in the service of Christ. It is good news that He is coming to execute perfect justice. His judgments are true and righteous (Rev. 19:2). Unlike earthly judges, He does not lack one shred of evidence, nor does He lack one ounce of wisdom.

The Great White Throne judgment of Revelation 20 speaks of a day when all of the dead will stand before the Lord to be judged according to what they have done. All injustice, unrighteousness, and wickedness will be brought to light. All people will be judged—believers and unbelievers—to eternal reward or eternal punishment. The idea that everything we have ever done will be exposed publicly is so distressing that some have argued believers will not be present at the final judgment. But the author of Hebrews counts this accounting as good news:

> And just as it is appointed for people to die once—and after this, judgment—so also Christ, having been offered once to bear the sins of many, will appear a second time, not to bear sin, but to bring salvation to those who are waiting for him. (Heb. 9:27–28)

For those in Christ, judgment is good news, as it ushers in the fullness of our salvation. We have nothing to dread in that accounting, because Christ has paid the penalty in full. We are forgetful and self-justifying by nature. We strive to repent of our known sins, but think how many unknown or forgotten or unacknowledged sins we will never confess in this lifetime? If anything, the full and public recounting of our offenses will complete our joy by showing us at last how high and long and wide and deep is the love of God in Christ for us.

When we live toward this future, we take our sin seriously today. And we take righteousness equally seriously. We count our salvation as dearly purchased, and in response, we "do justice, love kindness, and walk humbly" (Mic. 6:8 ESV) every day, in the here and now.

Our Comfort in a Kingdom without End

What happens next? The Christian story, from the very beginning, is moving toward the end. From the opening pages of Scripture, the scene was set. The tension was introduced, the conflict rose, the plot reached its climax, and the story moved inexorably toward its concluding scene: the kingdom of God finally and definitively established on earth.

John writes of this future and final scene in his vision. Upon seeing the new Jerusalem descend, he says: "Then I heard a loud voice from the throne: Look, God's dwelling is with humanity, and he will live with them. They will be his peoples, and God himself will be with them and will be their God. He will wipe away every tear from their eyes. Death will be no more; grief, crying, and pain will be no more, because the previous things have passed away" (Rev. 21:3–4). Christ the King is coming to dwell with us forever.

Note that God does not destroy His creation and start all over again. God is not coming to burn the earth up; He is coming to bring His kingdom down. He is coming to make all things new. The hope of the gospel is not simply that we escape the earth and go to heaven when we die. Though the intermediate state is comforting, it is not final. The message of the gospel is not salvation as escape, but salvation as restoration. God is not going to destroy all things. God is going to restore and resurrect all things. Our future hope is not only spiritual, but earthly. God is bringing heaven to earth.

Eschatology is not about destruction, but restoration. And God gets all the glory.

The End?

The end of the story is God dwelling with humanity forever. Until that day, rejoice in the hope that you have, because God has been merciful to us:

> He has given us new birth into a living hope through the resurrection of Jesus Christ from the dead and into an inheritance that is imperishable, undefiled, and unfading, kept in heaven for you. You are being guarded by God's power through faith for a salvation that is ready to be revealed in the last time. You rejoice in this, even though now for a short time, if necessary, you suffer grief in various trials so that the proven character of your faith—more valuable than gold which, though perishable, is refined by fire—may result in praise, glory, and honor at the revelation of Jesus Christ. (1 Pet. 1:3–7)

Our understanding of the story we're living in—from how it begins to how it ends—shapes every aspect of how we live. The Christian story gives us lives filled with meaning, purpose, value, contentment, and joy. We all live toward whatever end we believe is coming. The return of Christ is the perfect ending that makes yesterday, today, and tomorrow matter more than any other story.

If the grand conclusion of our story is Christ returning to dwell with His people forever, what should the posture of His people be today? The first and last instinct of Christian theologians is simple:

> Your kingdom come
> Your will be done
> *On earth* as it is in heaven.

Christian theologians are those who are beginning to learn that our greatest hope is God's kingdom *here*. God's will *here*. All theology is bound up in the hope for the King and His kingdom. And the good news is, that is *exactly* the hope Christ is coming back to fulfill.

The Bible ends with this beautiful promise, "He who testifies about these things says, 'Yes, I am coming soon.'"

And all Christian theologians respond: "Amen! Come, Lord Jesus!" (Rev. 22:20).

The best stories have the best endings. And the Christian story has the best ending of them all. Because the ending of the Bible is that Christ's kingdom never ends. We look forward to the return of Christ eagerly, not just because we love the kingdom, but because we love the King.

You Are a Theologian

Discuss

1. Before reading this chapter, how would you summarize your thoughts on eschatology in one sentence? After reading this chapter, how would you summarize your thoughts in one sentence?

2. We have asserted that the study of eschatology is intended to comfort the believer. Which of the issues discussed (bodily death, the return of Christ, the resurrection from the dead, final judgment, or kingdom without end) gives you the most comfort? Why? Which is hardest for you to see as comforting? Why?

3. How should understanding the earth as being remade versus destroyed impact the way we think about our stewardship of it?

4. How prone are you to an escapist view of Christ's return? How does an escapist mentality sabotage our ability to persevere in trial and work hard as unto the Lord in the here and now?

5. What is one insight you most want to remember about the end of the Christian story?

Pray

Focus on praying for today in light of our future hope. Meditate on each prayer statement below, adding specific ways to personalize it. Then pray the prayer aloud, adding your personal requests as you pray.

> *Lord, Thy kingdom come, Thy will be done in my thoughts.*
>
> *Lord, Thy kingdom come, Thy will be done in my words.*
>
> *Lord, Thy kingdom come, Thy will be done in my actions.*
>
> *Lord, Thy kingdom come, Thy will be done in my family.*
>
> *Lord, Thy kingdom come, Thy will be done in my friendships.*

Lord, Thy kingdom come, Thy will be done in my trials.

Lord, Thy kingdom come, Thy will be done in my work.

Lord, Thy kingdom come, Thy will be done in my leisure time.

Lord, Thy kingdom come, Thy will be done in my neighborhood.

Lord, Thy kingdom come, Thy will be done in my "Jerusalem."

Lord, Thy kingdom come, Thy will be done in my "Judea."

Lord, Thy kingdom come, Thy will be done "to the ends of the earth."

Lord, Thy kingdom come, Thy will be done in my church.

Lord, Thy kingdom come, Thy will be done in Your church.

Lord, Thy kingdom come, Thy will be done in my tomorrows.

Lord, Thy kingdom come, Thy will be done in the tomorrows I do not live to see.

CONCLUSION

Made You Look

Oh, there you are, turning that final page, looking for any last tidbits. If you've made it this far, we owe you a little bit of honesty.

First, this book has not made you a theologian. That's not because we have failed at our task, but because you already were one! We pray that this book helped you to grow as a Christian theologian—someone who delights in all of who God is and all that He has done. We pray it has introduced you to ideas that are new and has solidified for you ideas that were perhaps not new.

Second, this book has failed to answer all of your questions. Profoundly. But here's why: a good theologian finishes a book like this with more questions, not less. We knew that going in. Did you? This book is not intended to be a terminus for you, but a starting point. Keep going. Theology is the work of a lifetime, and the work of eternity, for that matter. Read your Bible, listen to sermons, read the footnotes of time-tested theologians, and follow every rabbit trail they introduce. Start meaningful conversations with other believers. Pursue humility. Keep an open mind. Strive to think critically without being critical in spirit. Take your time. Savor the journey.

Third, this book wants to change more than the way you think. It wants to travel from your head to your heart. While we hope that you learned about God and all that He has done, don't stop with learning. Discipleship begins with learning, but results in loving. Allow yourself to feel the significance and beauty of the truths you have learned. Ask the Spirit to transform your right thinking into right worship. Just as all of us are theologians, all of life is devoted to worship. Christian theologians set themselves the joyful task of learning to worship God as we ought, to the very best of our abilities, making the best use of the time, with the help of the Holy Spirit.

What Am I Supposed to Do Now?

Here is one thing we can guarantee is going to happen. You are going to start noticing theology is everywhere. You'll start to notice it in conversations, songs, movies, entertainment, and literature. It is everywhere, and it has always been there.

No, your pastor did not just start adding theology to his sermons. Yes, that worship lyric has always been like that. Yes, your favorite coffee mug has always taken that verse out of context.

What we don't want you to do is start being an arrogant theologian, because arrogance has no place in theology. Stay low. Stay humble. Keep learning. Theology leads us into Christlike humility.

Two of the best ways to keep learning theology in humility are to *read* and to *teach*. First, read Scripture. The Bible is the great school of theology. It is where all theology begins and ends. Don't neglect the formative nature of communing with God regularly through His Word. Maybe this means you should start a Bible study at your church or join one that already exists. Also, read great books. Read theologians, past and present, to gain greater wisdom from Christians who've gone before us. We can learn from both their insight and their folly.

Second, the best way to learn is to try to articulate to others what God is teaching you. If you only read this book, you won't remember much of it by next year. But if you try to talk about it with others, you will retain so much more. By teaching we don't mean you need to have a platform and microphone. This may look thousands of different ways. This may be a dad learning to articulate God's attributes to his son. It may be a woman on a walk with a neighbor talking about the nature of Scripture. It may be a teenager discussing the reality of sin with their grandparents. Theology is not just meant to be in our minds and hearts, but also on our lips. You can't teach what you don't know—so try to teach it! After all, the Great Commission is for everyone.

May God draw you ever closer to Himself as you daily seek His face. And may you yourself draw the next generation of disciples to become faithful theologians, teaching them to observe all He has commanded.

About the Authors

Jen Wilkin is a Bible teacher from Dallas, Texas. An advocate for Bible literacy, she has organized and led studies for women in home, church, and parachurch contexts. She has authored multiple Bible studies and books, including the bestseller, *Women of the Word: How to Study the Bible with Both Our Hearts and Our Minds*. You can find her at JenWilkin.net.

J. T. English, PhD, serves as a pastor, professor, and is the author of *Deep Discipleship: How the Local Church Can Make Whole Disciples*. J. T. is passionate about seeing God glorified through discipleship in the context of the local church.

He is also a cofounder of Training the Church, a ministry focused on assisting churches and ministry leaders develop and sustainable discipleship framework for their context. He is also cohost for *Knowing Faith*, a podcast that explores basic Christian beliefs. He received his ThM in Historical Theology from Dallas Theological Seminary and PhD in Systematic Theology from Southern Seminary.

Acknowledgments

We would like to thank Erik Wolgemuth and Wolgemuth & Associates for their steady, guiding hand. You make the world of publishing navigable for two very busy people.

Thank you to Devin Maddox, Mary Wiley, Erin Ivey, Stacey Sapp, Whitney Alexander, Ashley Gorman, Kim Stanford, and the entire B&H Publishing team at Lifeway. Your patience and professionalism set you apart. You believed in this project and lent it your prodigious gifts. We could not ask for better ministry partners.

We are thankful to The Village Church for saying "yes" to the reclamation of Christian discipleship in the local church setting. They believed it was possible, and they committed to the vision of both men and women flourishing in that space.

We are also both deeply grateful for our ministry colleague Kyle Worley. He helped us build theological education in the local church and continues to be a strong advocate for the importance of charitable theological discourse on our podcast, *Knowing Faith*.

I (J. T.) would like to thank my wife, Macy, for her steady faithfulness in following Jesus through every season. I never could have undertaken this ministry calling without her. She is the best wife, mom, and theologian I know because she follows Jesus wherever He leads. My children and I will forever be grateful for her Christlike example and encouragement in our lives. I am also indebted to Storyline Church and The Village Church. Both churches gave me the opportunity to lead with a theological vision for ministry, and my prayer is that both churches remain faithful to the gospel of Jesus Christ until He returns. Finally, I am deeply grateful to my most formative teachers, Dr. D. Jeffrey Bingham and Dr. Gregg Allison for helping spark my love for theology and the local church. They have embodied, for me, what it means to be a theologian. Thank you.

I (Jen) would like to thank my husband, Jeff, for the gift of that systematic theology text in February 1999. In many ways, it's the story of our thirty years together. You tell me I can do it, and then you tell me that I should and that I must. And then you stand beside me to help me get it done. The world will never know how many drafts you have listened to me read aloud, how many teachings you have patiently heard me hash out before they ever find their form. But I will always know. You are my favorite.

Notes

1. https://thestateoftheology.com/

2. We would be remiss not to mention the third member of our team who shares this vision for discipleship, our faithful brother Kyle Worley. With him, we have worked to carry what we learned in our local church to other local churches around the world through the ministry Training the Church and the *Knowing Faith* podcast.

3. Jen Wilkin, *Women of the Word: How to Study the Bible with Both Our Hearts and Our Minds* (Wheaton, IL: Crossway, 2019), 31.

4. Jen Wilkin, *None Like Him: 10 Ways God Is Different from Us* (Wheaton, IL: Crossway, 2016).

5. Definitions are adapted from *Romans 2: An In-depth Inductive Study That Will Help You Understand God's Word, Bring Healing to Your Soul, and Give You Direction (Precept Upon Precept)* (Precept Ministries International, 2007).

6. John Calvin, *Institutes*, Book 1, Chapter 1, www.reformed.org/books/institutes/books/book1/bk1ch01.html.

7. J. I. Packer, et al., "Infallibility," *New Dictionary of Theology* (Downers Grove, IL: InterVarsity Press, 1988).

8. Jen Wilkin, *In His Image: 10 Ways God Calls Us to Reflect His Character* (Wheaton, IL: Crossway, 2018), 128.

9. Nicene Creed, fourth-centery version found at https://www. fourthcentury.com/urkunde-24/.

10. Matthew Schmitz, "Texas Bible Converts 'You' to 'Ya'll,'" First Things, June 3, 2013, https://www.firstthings.com/blogs/ firstthoughts/2013/06/texas-bible-converts-you-to-yall.

11. Alistair Begg, "The Main Things Are the Plain Things," YouTube, https://www.youtube.com/watch?v=Rg5N1J5qk3A.

OTHER RESOURCES
by Jen Wilkin

ABIDE
10 Sessions

See how 1, 2, and 3 John compel Christians to recall a great salvation and abide in truth.

BETTER
10 Sessions

Explore the book of Hebrews to learn how to place your hope and faith in Christ alone.

GOD OF CREATION
10 Sessions

Learn how the first 11 chapters of Genesis set the scene for the story of the Bible as a whole.

GOD OF COVENANT
10 Sessions

Witness God's faithfulness in Genesis 12–50 to Abraham, Isaac, Jacob, and Joseph, and discern Christ in the stories of His people.

1 PETER
9 Sessions

Study the book of 1 Peter to look beyond your current circumstances to a future inheritance through Christ.

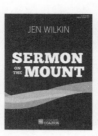

SERMON ON THE MOUNT
9 Sessions

Study Jesus's sermon on the mount verse by verse to learn what it means to be a citizen of the kingdom of heaven.

Lifeway women

Available wherever books are sold.